The Sacred Writings
of Paul

Books in the
SkyLight Illuminations Series

Bhagavad Gita: Annotated & Explained

The Book of Mormon: Selections Annotated & Explained

Dhammapada: Annotated & Explained

*The Divine Feminine in Biblical Wisdom Literature:
    Selections Annotated & Explained*

*The End of Days: Essential Selections from
    Apocalyptic Texts—Annotated & Explained*

Gnostic Writings on the Soul: Annotated & Explained

The Gospel of Philip: Annotated & Explained

The Gospel of Thomas: Annotated & Explained

Hasidic Tales: Annotated & Explained

The Hebrew Prophets: Selections Annotated & Explained

The Hidden Gospel of Matthew: Annotated & Explained

*The Lost Sayings of Jesus: Teachings from Ancient Christian,
    Jewish, Gnostic, and Islamic Sources—Annotated & Explained*

Native American Stories of the Sacred: Annotated & Explained

*Philokalia: The Eastern Christian Spiritual Texts—
    Selections Annotated & Explained*

*The Qur'an and Sayings of Prophet Muhammad:
    Selections Annotated & Explained*

*Rumi and Islam: Selections from His Stories, Poems, and Discourses—
    Annotated & Explained*

The Sacred Writings of Paul: Selections Annotated & Explained

The Secret Book of John: The Gnostic Gospel—Annotated & Explained

Selections from the Gospel of Sri Ramakrishna: Annotated & Explained

Sex Texts from the Bible: Selections Annotated & Explained

Spiritual Writings on Mary: Annotated & Explained

Tao Te Ching: Annotated & Explained

The Way of a Pilgrim: Annotated & Explained

Zohar: Annotated & Explained

The Sacred Writings of Paul

Annotated & Explained

Translation & Annotation by Ron Miller

Walking Together, Finding the Way ®
SKYLIGHT PATHS®
PUBLISHING
Woodstock, Vermont

The Sacred Writings of Paul:
Selections Annotated & Explained

2007 First Printing
Translations, annotation, and introductory material © 2007 by Ron Miller

For information regarding permission to reprint material from this book, please mail or fax your request in writing to SkyLight Paths Publishing, Permissions Department, at the address / fax number listed below, or e-mail your request to permissions@ skylightpaths.com.

Library of Congress Cataloging-in-Publication Data
Miller, Ron, 1938–
  The sacred writings of Paul : selections annotated & explained / translation & annotation by Ron Miller.
       p. cm.—(Skylight illuminations series)
  Includes bibliographical references.
  ISBN-13: 978-1-59473-213-3 (quality pbk.)
  ISBN-10: 1-59473-213-2 (quality pbk.)
  1. Paul, the Apostle, Saint. 2. Bible. N.T. Epistles of Paul—Criticism, interpretation, etc. 3. Bible. N.T. Epistles of Paul—Theology. I. Title.

BS2506.3.M55 2007
227'.05209—dc22

                                                                        2007001795

10   9   8   7   6   5   4   3   2   1

Manufactured in the United States of America

Cover design: Walter C. Bumford III
Cover art: *St. Paul* by Elizabeth Hudgins © 1997 by Elizabeth Hudgins

SkyLight Paths Publishing is creating a place where people of different spiritual traditions come together for challenge and inspiration, a place where we can help each other understand the mystery that lies at the heart of our existence.

SkyLight Paths sees both believers and seekers as a community that increasingly transcends traditional boundaries of religion and denomination—people wanting to learn from each other, *walking together, finding the way*.

SkyLight Paths, "Walking Together, Finding the Way" and colophon are trademarks of LongHill Partners, Inc., registered in the U.S. Patent and Trademark Office.

Walking Together, Finding the Way®
Published by SkyLight Paths® Publishing
A Division of LongHill Partners, Inc.
Sunset Farm Offices, Route 4, P.O. Box 237
Woodstock, VT 05091
Tel: (802) 457-4000   Fax: (802) 457-4004
www.skylightpaths.com

To my good friend,
Lois,
Who brings laughter and sunshine
To all she meets.
She is the kind of friend
Everyone should have.

Contents ☐

Introduction   ix
Acknowledgments   xlv
A Note on the Translation   xlvii

1. Paul on Paul   1

2. Sin and Grace   17

3. Old and New Creation   35

4. The Call to Community   45

5. The Lord's Supper   89

6. Jews and Christians   97

7. Teachings on Sexuality   121

8. Love   135

9. The End Times   147

10. God's Plan for the Jews   163

Suggestions for Further Reading   170
Index of Bible Passages Annotated   171

Introduction ☐

The second most important person in the founding, growth, and ongoing development of Christianity is Paul of Tarsus, often referred to as Saint Paul or the Apostle Paul. Over the years of researching, writing, and teaching about Jesus and his message, I have found myself increasingly drawn to know more about this man. I am by no means alone in this; recently, there has been a groundswell of interest in this figure who had so much influence in charting the centuries-long course of one of the world's great faiths. With the sole exception of Jesus, more books have been written about Paul than about any other figure related to Christianity.

Any investigation of Paul will soon come up against three questions that loom large, both with reference to Paul himself and with regard to his continuing legacy in the Christian church. First, how alike or unlike were Jesus and Paul? Second, if there were differences between them, what effect did that have on the growth of Christianity? And third, how can these differences, if they do indeed exist, help Christians today in finding their way forward in the midst of countless new and creative ways of understanding their religion and their spirituality?

Answering these questions for ourselves can help us assess Paul in light of our own historical and cultural situation. In this book, I explore the following answers to these three critical questions. First, Jesus and Paul were in fact unlike in many ways. Second, their differences did indeed have a tremendous impact on how Christianity developed. And third, understanding those differences can help move Christianity into a future faithful to its deepest truth. My hope is that this book will offer the reader guidance in understanding the importance of these three questions; additional insight into their answers; and, stemming from that insight, wisdom in shaping the future course of Christian theology and spirituality.

How Alike or Unlike Were Jesus and Paul?

Jesus (circa 4 B.C.E. to 30 C.E.) and Paul (circa 2 B.C.E. to 67 C.E.) lived in roughly the same time frame but never met. Jesus taught for only three years, beginning when he was about thirty years old. We know little to nothing about the first thirty years of his life, his so-called hidden years, and as far as we know, as an adult his travels were limited to his Jewish homeland. He was executed as a political criminal by the Roman Empire when he was in his early thirties.

Paul, on the other hand, missionized more years than Jesus lived, traveled widely throughout the Roman world, and was in his seventies when he, too, was executed by the Roman Empire. By then he had traveled thousands of miles, finally meeting his death in the very capital of the empire.

Jesus and Paul were both Jews, believed in the same God, and grew up within the structure of the same religion. The most significant difference between them, however, lies in the fact that Jesus was a Palestinian Jew, whereas Paul was a Hellenistic Jew.

Hellas is the Greek word for Greece. Things Greek are Hellenic. Hellenism, on the other hand, refers to the mixing of Greek and Mideastern cultures that began with the conquests of Alexander the Great, who swept from Macedonia and Greece in the fourth century B.C.E. to conquer cities and kingdoms as far east as present-day India. Artists and architects, poets and philosophers, not only soldiers, accompanied Alexander's conquests.

The Greek language became the common language of the conquered territories. The landmarks of Greek culture—the gymnasium, temple, and theater—advertised Alexander's program. The gymnasium, in particular, was a central institution. It was a place where free men exercised their bodies (the root meaning of the word *gymnasium* is "naked") but then, unlike in American gyms, entered classrooms where they could attend lectures, poetry readings, and musical performances. This is why the highest form of secondary school in Germany is called a *Gymnasium*, a usage that often puzzles American visitors.

When the Roman Empire replaced Hellenistic rule, Romans brought expertise and advancements in many areas: the organization of armies, the codification of laws, and architectural achievements of practical import, such as well-built roads and extraordinarily designed aqueducts. And yet, the superiority of the Greek language and the sophistication of Greek cultural achievements were recognized and preserved by the Romans. Wealthy Romans sent their sons to Greek universities and had Greek slaves to tutor them at home.

Unlike the Greeks who named their country Hellas, Palestine was a name given to biblical Israel by the foreign empires ruling there. Palestinian Jews were not unaffected by Greek influence, but it was far less pervasive than in the cities outside Israel. Herod the Great, whom the Romans allowed to rule in Palestine as a puppet king until his death in 4 B.C.E., attempted to further spread the Hellenism of his Roman masters in the southern part of Palestine called Judea.

His son, Herod Antipas, a client king in the Galilee at the time of Jesus's public life (27–30 C.E.), tried to emulate his father by bringing that Hellenistic influence into the northern territory of the Galilee. He built a palace and a theater that seated three thousand people in Sepphoris, a city just a ten-minute walk from Jesus's hometown, the small farming community of Nazareth.

But despite the efforts of Herod the Great and his son, Herod Antipas, the Hellenistic influence was, in most cases, limited and superficial, especially outside the larger urban centers. The vernacular language in Palestine was Aramaic, not Greek, although Jews having frequent contact with their Gentile overlords undoubtedly spoke Greek. In general, however, the Greek cultural influence did not run deep among most Palestinian Jews. Nine out of ten Jews were dirt-poor peasants who, in their daily struggle for survival, had little interest in the niceties of Hellenistic thought.

Jesus was one of those peasants. He taught in Aramaic, a language close to Hebrew, and never wrote anything. In fact, most scholars doubt that he was able to write, and some even question his ability to read. Jesus spent his life in villages of poor farmers or fishermen, except for the few times that celebrating the Jewish holidays brought him to Jerusalem. He probably never traveled more than seventy miles from the little town where he was born. Matthew's account of the flight to Egypt when Jesus was a baby is viewed as midrash (homiletic commentary on scriptural passages) rather than factual history by most scholars of the Christian Testament.

Tarsus, Paul's birthplace, was a Hellenistic city, and Paul was a Hellenistic Jew. He probably knew both Aramaic and Hebrew but had Greek as his native tongue, a language he wrote in with great eloquence. Not only did he write his letters in Greek, but he also quoted the Hebrew Bible from the Septuagint version, the translation into Greek made by the Jews in Egyptian Alexandria some two hundred years earlier. Paul wore his hair short and was clean shaven; he considered long hair on men to be unnatural (1 Cor. 11:14). He was familiar with Greek poetry, theater, and the games that were part of the great celebrations (like our Olympic Games today).

Paul was also affected by the current Greek philosophy, especially the influence of Plato. Platonic thought saw human beings as composed of two distinct entities: a body and a soul. The body went into the grave after death, but the soul set out on its immortal journey. As a Jew, Paul could not accept this strict Platonic view of a divided human nature. Hence, Paul taught the resurrection of the body—albeit a "spiritual body"—that combined these strands of Jewish and Greek thought into something of a paradox. Such tensions are characteristic of many of Paul's teachings.

Jesus was not exposed to this kind of dualistic thinking. In the thought and language of the Hebrew Bible, the human person is one. There is no word in Hebrew or Aramaic for a separate soul entity. One of Jesus's teachings, recorded in Greek and rendered in English translation, reads: "What does it profit a man to gain the whole world and lose his soul?" This teaching is found in Matthew, Mark, and Luke.

Soul is the correct English word to translate the Greek, but since Jesus taught in Aramaic, a less Hellenistic translation might be: "What does it profit people to gain the whole world at the expense of what is deepest in them?"

This same Hellenistic dualism, affecting Paul but not Jesus, led in the former to an understandable disparagement of the material world. The material world, like the body, was all part of that inferior realm that was left behind when the soul soared to God. Even during this present life, material reality was more of a hindrance than a help in the Hellenistic mind-set. In some forms of Greek thought, the material world is despicable, even evil.

Paul's Jewishness prevented him from going that far. After all, the God of his tradition looks at creation and pronounces it "very good" (Gen. 1:31). Nevertheless, Paul often portrayed the material world as but a pale reflection of the spiritual world.

Things were different with Jesus, who was not a Hellenistic Jew. Knowing no Greek, wearing a beard, and having long hair, Jesus never saw a play or attended civic games. But as a Galilean peasant, unaffected by the philosophies of Greece, Jesus was deeply immersed in the world around him, marveling at fields of wildflowers, women baking bread, and farmers and fishermen busy in their work. Jesus saw in these worldly experiences direct links to the spiritual world.

The difference between Jesus and Paul in their attitude to the physical world is illustrated by the fact that in none of the fourteen letters in the Christian Testament attributed to him does Paul ever describe a sunrise in Corinth or the beauty of the countryside through which he walked so many years.

Another difference between Jesus and Paul can be illustrated by two divergent paradigms of spiritual growth: blessed participation on the one hand, and holy abstinence on the other. Jesus's spirituality was based in blessed participation; Paul's, in holy abstinence.

Blessed participation is rooted in the Jewish theology of blessing. Every blessing consists of two parts: a reference to the transcendence of

xiv **Introduction**

God (Blessed are You, Lord God, Ruler of the Universe) and a reference to some action in human experience—eating bread, drinking wine, or seeing a wonder of nature. We experience God as the horizon in which these activities take place. One's life becomes a series of blessings through participation in the moment-to-moment encounters with the day's events.

From the perspective of this paradigm, the world is good. It is not an obstacle on the way to God; it is the way. And it is precisely through our participation in the world that we know God.

Holy abstinence, on the other hand, is rooted in a dualistic view of the world in which the path to God is like climbing a ladder. At the bottom of the ladder we find matter, body, and woman. At the top of the ladder we find spirit, soul, and man. The more we abstain from the lower, the more quickly we attain to the higher. Being sexually abstinent is better than being sexually active. Fasting is better than enjoying food and drink.

Palestinian Judaism tended toward blessed participation. Hellenistic Judaism, on the other hand, paved the way for Christianity's embracing of holy abstinence. I remember being a bit stunned when one of my graduate school teachers pointed out that in the Palestinian Talmud (a multivolume commentary on the Torah) we are taught that we will be called to account by God on judgment day for every joy of creation in which we failed to participate. When I asked the professor to repeat the quote, he was aware of my surprise and said, "Don't worry. You're just thinking like a Christian." My Hellenistic heritage was thus revealed to the whole class. As a Christian, I bore the influence of Paul, whereas the ancient Jewish text was more consonant with the spirituality of Jesus.

How Did These Differences Affect Christianity's Development?

The model of holy abstinence, reflecting Hellenistic thought, clearly predominated in Christianity's early development. Celibacy, for example, became normative for Christians seriously committed to a spiritual life. And this despite the fact that we have no clear evidence that either Jesus or Paul was celibate. Recent scholarship on Mary Magdalene suggests that she may have been Jesus's life partner; as a Pharisee, Paul would certainly have fulfilled the commandment to marry. Scholars speculate that he was either divorced or widowed when we meet him in his letters.

Zealous Christians competed in climbing higher on the ladder to holiness. Some of the fourth-century monastics refrained from even the simple pleasure of looking at the stream that ran by their cave; others slept standing up, leaning on a ledge, rather than reclining on a sleeping mat. Then there were the Stylites, or Pillar Saints, who lived upon the ruins of structures or on the top of columns or pillars, standing there day and night in order to proclaim their Christianity by giving up physical movement itself.

Being the synthesis of both Hebrew spirituality via Jesus and Hellenistic philosophy via Paul, Christian spirituality often reflects the tension between these paradigms. For many centuries, it was acceptable for married couples to be sexually active but only for the sake of procreation, not physical intimacy. It was all right to eat and drink but only to nourish you to do God's work in the world, not for the sheer joy of shared food. These attitudes are beginning to change, but even today Lenten practice often revolves around what we're "giving up for Lent," and we have lingering notions that God is somehow more pleased by what we give up than by what we enjoy.

How Can These Differences Lead Christianity Forward?
There is a tendency in Christian scholarship today to focus on the scholarly reconstruction of the authentic teachings of Jesus as the starting point of Christian theology. But this was not always the case. Earlier scholars, such as Martin Luther, began with the premise that it was Paul who best understood Jesus. Thus, Luther (and many of the theologians who followed him on this point) had, for example, a low regard for the Letter of James in the Christian canon because it seemed at variance with the teachings of Paul.

Scholars today are finding a new interest in this letter attributed to Jesus's brother, who headed up the mother church in Jerusalem for some thirty years. There are more similarities to Jesus's teachings in this short letter than in all the letters of Paul combined. So Luther was right in one way and wrong in another. He accurately noted that the Letter of James was not like Paul's letters. What he failed to notice, however, was how remarkably close this letter was to some of the explicit teachings of Jesus.

It's evident that the choice of a starting point shapes the theology that finally emerges. It has often been said that if you scratch a Christian, you find more of Paul than of Jesus. If that is indeed the case, then it follows that much of Christian theology and spiritual practice may need to be revised, or at least revisited.

We've already discussed the Hellenistic thinking underlying much of Christian thinking as stemming more from Paul than from Jesus. But if instead Christians today began with Jesus instead of Paul, they might find new freedom in a spirituality of blessed participation, bringing with it new theological understandings and new forms of spiritual practice. For example, one day, Catholic priests could be married men and women. Both homosexual and heterosexual love could be celebrated. "Impure thoughts" could be understood as useful fantasies and masturbation regarded as a healthy form of sexual expression. Healthy eating, physical exercise, and bodily disciplines (such as hatha yoga or tai chi) could be seen as integral parts of a spiritual regimen.

Jesus regarded human nature as good and open to God's reign. Jesus was loose about religion but tight about God. The religious differences between his fellow Jews and the Roman officers in his homeland seemed of less importance to him than people's hearts, their essential openness to the Divine. This might counter some of the exclusivism we find in Paul's message, helping Christian communities to become open and more welcoming, eager to learn from participants in other sacred traditions, regarding practioners of other religions as allies rather than as adversaries Deep dialogue, rather than the diatribe so common in Paul, will be the norm of Christian life and practice. This focus on Christianity's future will be a recurring theme in the body of this book.

A Sketch of Paul's Life

The path to Paul is paved with paradox. Paul was a work in progress. He did not stand still long enough to be readily categorized. He could be flying at a mystic level of consciousness in one minute and then, in the next minute, suddenly descend to petty bickering. He was capable of demonstrating compassion and love in one sentence and betraying a thin-skinned defensiveness in the next. He could move from startlingly incisive arguments to illogical diatribes without skipping a beat. He was consistent only in his inconsistency, comforting in one moment and criticizing in the next, continually conflicted in ways beyond counting. He was, above all else, one-of-a-kind Paul.

Dichotomies and dualisms dot the landscape of his writings. It was often when opposing adversaries that Paul seemed most able to articulate what he was supporting. The diatribe that, in antiquity, was an important rhetorical device for opposing adversaries was a frequently used weapon in Paul's arsenal. True dialogue, as we understand it today, was virtually absent in Paul's writings.

Neither a calm philosopher nor a rational academician, Paul was nonetheless a brilliant thinker who drew upon all his available sources in a multitude of ways to support his always developing vision of life and the Christian faith. On a personal level, he was a man beset by a host of trials, a fighter struggling with a variety of enemies, a compassionate servant of God supported by loyal friends whose affection for him was boundless.

Paul was born around 2 B.C.E. in Tarsus, a city found today in eastern Turkey. He had two names: Saul, his Hebrew name, and Paul, his Roman name, since his father was a Roman citizen. (Jesus, on the other hand, had only one name: Jehoshua Ben Josef, Joshua the son of Joseph; the shorter form of his name was Jeshu, which in Greek translation becomes Jesus.)

Jewish and Greek thought flowed together in Paul's education in Tarsus. He probably continued his studies in Jerusalem, pursuing his Jewish life as a Pharisee, part of a community of conscientious Jews praying and studying together and sharing table fellowship. While dedicating most of his time to these religious pursuits, he learned to support himself by making tents.

Not comfortable with tolerating Jews who were joining the new Jesus movement, Paul was allied with Jewish authorities wanting to punish these apostates. But suddenly, in the year 33 c.e., his whole world was turned upside down when he was transformed from persecutor to propagator of the new faith by a personal revelation of the Risen Christ.

This was the pivotal event in Paul's life. He refers to it in his own writings, though with no details. Luke fills in those details in describing this event several times in Acts: Paul falling from his horse, the blinding light, the voice of the Risen Christ asking Paul why he was persecuting him. Paul sought out the Christian community in Damascus after this experience for basic instruction and baptism, then moved on to pursue missionary work among the Gentiles of Arabia (modern Jordan and parts of Iraq). He went back to Damascus at some point but left there again in 37 c.e. to travel to Jerusalem.

It was there that Paul had the opportunity to meet some of Jesus's disciples, especially Simon Peter and Jesus's brother, James. Paul wrote that he spent fifteen days there with Peter and James (Gal. 1:18). Paul was undoubtedly eager to form bonds of unity with those who had known Jesus during his earthly ministry. But he's very clear about the fact that these disciples of Jesus were not the source of his mission to the Gentiles; that had come from the Risen Christ and him alone.

At some point, Paul fell ill. He settled in the Celtic territory of Galatia and did missionary work there while he recovered. We don't know the nature of this illness, but some scholars surmise that it may have had something to do with his eyesight, because he wrote to the Galatians: "You would have torn out your eyes and given them to me" (Gal. 4:15). Paul was thankful for the Galatians' generosity in nursing him back to health, and many of them became his most loyal followers.

By 48 c.e. Paul made his way to Troas, a city on the Aegean coast of Asia Minor, a handy springboard to the cities of Greece. Paul crossed the

Aegean and reached modern-day Europe, establishing churches in Phillipi, Thessalonica, and Corinth. His missionary tactics in these Greek cities resulted in his having to go back to Jerusalem to defend his understanding of the Gospel, the basic good news of Christianity. Paul wrote that this trip occurred fourteen years after his earlier visit, thus in 51 c.e. (Gal. 2:1).

Why did Paul have to go back to Jerusalem? His views on how Jewish one had to be to become a Christian were making him a lot of enemies. Implicit in Paul's approach was a distinction between two categories of instruction found in the Torah: moral laws and holiness codes. When a moral law is violated, it is called a sin. The hallmark of a violation of a moral law is that someone is physically or emotionally hurt—as in murder, theft, adultery, or bearing false witness.

When a holiness code is violated, however, it is called an abomination (the root meaning suggests some kind of forbidden mixing). The hallmark of a violation of a holiness code is that the integrity of the community is somehow violated—working on the Sabbath, eating pork, wearing linen and wool at the same time, a man having sexual relations with a man, a woman having sexual relations with an animal, and eating creatures that are themselves mixtures of fish and animal (such as lobsters and crabs). Such "abominations" violated the criteria by which Jews were to be identified as a distinct people—a holy people, a people set apart.

In Galatians 5:14, Paul told his readers that "the whole Torah is summed up in a single commandment, 'You shall love your neighbor as yourself' [Lev. 19:18]." In other words, the moral codes constituted the essence of the Torah. To us today, it seems self-evident that loving our neighbor is more important, more moral, and even more godly than not wearing linen and wool at the same time.

And yet, what was innovative and what some might have seen as liberating in Paul's practice was precisely what disturbed his Jewish-Christian opponents. He was telling Gentile converts that they were bound by the moral laws, which he understood to be eternal, but they were not bound by the holiness codes, which, according to Paul, were meant to guide the people from Sinai to the coming of the Messiah. Now that the Messiah had come and was reigning with God, the holiness codes had no further relevance for Jews or Gentiles. Jews may continue to practice them out of habit—someone who has never eaten pork may not be anxious to begin doing so—but they no longer had any relevance for being healed, made whole and holy—that is, with being saved. Without Paul's declaration that Gentiles could circumvent the Jewish tradition and become Christians directly, Christianity would probably have remained a Jewish sect and the Christian church as we know it today would never have come into being.

The term for those Christians who disagreed with Paul on these matters, arguing that Gentile converts must keep both the moral and the holiness precepts, was *Judaizers*. They figure prominently in Paul's letters. No one at that time knew the consequences of settling that debate in favor of the Judaizers or in favor of Paul. But the Christian community in Antioch that had been supporting Paul's missionary ventures saw how these diverse views were splitting the community, so they sent Paul, along with Barnabas and Titus (a Gentile convert to Christianity), to consult with the mother church in Jerusalem. Paul went to Jerusalem unaware of how much hung in the balance.

James (Jesus's brother) headed up the Jerusalem community of Christians, and Paul knew that his understanding of the mission to the Gentiles had no chance of surviving without the approval of James. And so it was that some time in 51 c.e., Paul and his little delegation met with James.

Although Paul's missionary tactics were most likely disturbing to James, he could not help but recognize Paul's sincerity and conviction. We don't know which arguments convinced James to disagree with the Judaizers and take his stand with Paul, but Paul himself wrote that the leaders in Jerusalem gave him "the right hand of fellowship" (Gal. 2:9), agreeing that Paul had a legitimate mission to the Gentiles just as the Jerusalem church had a responsibility to extend its message to the Jews. A sign of Paul's goodwill was his commitment to raise funds for the poor in the mother church.

Antioch, a city north of Jerusalem on the way to Asia Minor (modern Turkey), was an important center of the Jesus movement. Paul's delegation returned happily to the church at Antioch, their home church and base of operation. But their homecoming was not a honeymoon. Peter, who had never lived in a mixed community of Jewish and Gentile Christians, came to pay a visit.

At first, the mood was irenic, and Peter agreed to share table fellowship with the Gentile Christians, thereby neglecting the rules of kashrut (holiness codes determining which foods could be eaten and how they should be prepared). But when some visitors came from the Jerusalem church (no doubt Judaizers), Peter gave way to the pressure and went back to eating only with Jewish Christians at separate kosher tables.

This hit a nerve for Paul. Few things seemed to annoy Paul more than seeing his Gentile converts treated like second-class citizens, and Peter's decision to no longer eat with them was a clear insult. Peter's action elicited strong words from Paul, who accused Peter and those who joined him of hypocrisy: "And the other Jews [Jewish Christians] joined him in this hypocrisy, so that even Barnabas was led astray by their hypocrisy" (Gal. 2:11).

What a blow this must have been for Paul. He lost Peter's support, as well as that of his longtime friend and missionary companion, Barnabas. Paul left Antioch. He never returned, nor did he make any further mention of Barnabas. By ending his relationship with Antioch, Paul lost his home church and the community that gave his mission legitimacy. He was then on his own, with only his beloved coworker, Timothy, still at his side.

Paul's next letter was to the Galatians, and he let them know from the first verse that his status as an ambassador (a word that is normally translated as "apostle") of the Risen Christ came directly from that same Christ and from God the Father (Gal. 1:1). After writing to them, he went in person, spending the summer of 52 c.e. among them. After that recuperative summer, Paul and Timothy covered well over three hundred miles to get to Ephesus.

Ephesus was the capital of the Roman province of Asia (thus the term *Asia Minor*, which is Turkey today) and an extremely important center of communication between the western and the eastern provinces. (I recently visited the site of this ancient city. Even today, walking on the stone roads through its ruins, one cannot help but sense its former grandeur.)

Ephesus eventually became the center from which packets of Paul's letters were sent around the Roman world. In fact, the canonical Letter to the Ephesians, although most likely penned by a disciple of Paul, not Paul himself, probably functioned as a cover letter for the bundles of Paul's writings prepared for shipping. The Letter to the Ephesians served as a summary of Paul's basic teachings, preparing the readers for what they would find in the enclosed correspondence.

Paul spent more than two years in Ephesus and used it as his base for maintaining contact with the churches he had already established, as well as a place from which to launch new missionary endeavors. While there, he sent his own delegation of followers to Philippi and Colossae to further propagate his understanding of the Gospel. Paul's goal was to bring his saving message to as many cities of the Roman Empire as possible—from Antioch to Galatia to Ephesus to Corinth to Rome to Spain to Northern Africa.

By 56 C.E., Paul had accomplished as much, if not more, than most people do in a lifetime. He was in his sixties by then, and it was time to deliver to James the money he had promised to collect for the poor of Jerusalem. Paul was naturally apprehensive about his reception in Jerusalem, especially after the debacle in Antioch five years earlier. If the Jerusalem church received the offerings of Paul, collected by Gentiles who were struggling against the Judaizers, then the mother church would be intrinsically tied to Paul's churches and would, in effect, approve of Paul's methods.

Reaching Jerusalem in 56 C.E., Paul had to win the good graces of the mother church. Paul tactfully agreed to undergo the purification required of all Jews coming from pagan territory and wanting to enter the Temple. But before any of that could happen, some non-Christian

Jews tried to kill Paul. Some alert Roman soldiers saw what was going on and rescued Paul from his would-be assassins. But a nervous Roman procurator, Felix, afraid of Jewish reprisals, sentenced Paul to prison in the maritime city of Caesarea, where Paul remained for two years.

A new procurator, Porcius Festus, was appointed by Rome in 58 C.E. Although Paul tried to defend himself, Festus, acting like his predecessor out of fear of Jewish protests, decided to avoid any responsibility by sending Paul to Rome to be judged by the emperor. Paul was found innocent by a Roman court and in 62 C.E. found himself once again a free man. With indefatigable zeal, he set out on another journey to numerous cities in the empire.

It was June of 64 C.E. when a fire swept through Rome. By the time it had played itself out, ten of the city's fourteen regions had been destroyed. The Roman emperor Nero decided to use Rome's Christian population as a scapegoat for the fire and for other problems in his administration as well. Nero had rewritten the laws so that simply being a Christian was an offense. Persecutions broke out everywhere.

When the persecutions subsided by 65 C.E., Paul apparently felt safe enough to return to Rome to strengthen the Christians who had survived Nero's wrath. Nevertheless, the new law led to his arrest, and Paul once again was sent to prison. In 67 C.E., his case was finally brought before the magistrate, and the mere fact that he acknowledged that he was a Christian led to a guilty judgment and a death sentence. Like Jesus before him, Paul was found guilty and condemned to death by a Roman authority. This stalwart soldier of Christ, then an old man in his seventies, was beheaded. Like his Master, he died proclaiming God's reign in the face of Caesar's empire.

God's Word vs. God's Words

As we prepare to study these passages from Paul's letters, we need to consider the ways in which these texts are regarded as inspired or sacred. A related question is the manner and degree of authority the Bible has over our lives. Not surprisingly, faithful Christians can and do have divergent opinions on such matters. For example, it is common in many churches for the reader to say, "This is the Word of the Lord" after reading a text from scripture. In other churches, the reader may say, "These are the Words of the Lord." The difference is small but significant, for in these two expressions we find encapsulated two distinct approaches to the sacred text.

When we say, "This is the Word of the Lord," we are stating our belief that this text, read publicly in solemn assembly, gives us an inspired message both to ponder and to include in our walk of faith. But this approach also allows that the text itself was written by human beings and reflects the sociological, economic, political, scientific, and psychological limitations both of the author as an individual and of the society in which the author was writing.

In this view, the text, like any human text, is partial, provisional, and perspectival. It is partial because no text can contain all that could be said. John's Gospel ends with a verse telling us that what is written there is true, "But there are also many other things that Jesus did; if every one of them were written down, I suppose that the world itself could not contain the books that would be written" (John 21:25).

The partial character of the text implies its provisional nature as well. Because there are limitations in the author—Paul, for example, nowhere condemns the institution of slavery—subsequent knowledge allows our understanding to grow. Certainly we can presume that Paul would have learned a few things in two thousand years. Current knowledge of the evils of slavery, the subtleties of gender inequality, insights into the nature of sexual orientation, the power of dialogue and how it differs from the diatribe that was frequently used by Paul, and many other such issues challenge us to carry the text forward with us, critically examining where Paul spoke from his genuine connection to God's Spirit and where, despite his own assertions to the contrary, his words were the product of the limitations of his time, culture, and geography. The work of discerning the Word of God cannot be relegated to Paul alone; it is our responsbility to continue that work in our own day and in our own circumstances, bearing in mind that ultimately we, too, are limited.

Finally, the text is perspectival. Men see the world differently than women do, rich people see it differently than do poor people, employers see it differently than employees do—the list is endless. One of my college philosophy professors reminded us one day that we don't have the option to be free from biases, but we do have the option to have some awareness of them. The biblical authors are no less subject to biases than anyone else who has ever lived. Paul was sometimes wrong, but this doesn't mean that he was always wrong. When it comes to the Word of God, despite what some may have us believe, there's more gray than black and white. Indeed, even the idea of "black and white," "all or nothing" is dualism in action, part of Paul's heritage to Christian orthodoxy.

If, however, we see the text as the Words of God, then we are in quite a different place. Such words are conceived as directly dictated by God to a human author, who in this case functions pretty much as a secretary taking dictation. The Words of God are presumed to be infallible and inerrant. And this includes words about any subject: the age of the world, the structure of the family, or even the nature of drunkenness. In the first model, the Word of God begins a discussion. Later insights about the given topic must be incorporated into our understanding of the text. In the second model, the Words of God end the discussion. For how can anything be added to words God has spoken?

It will be clear to the reader from page one of this book which model I am following. I believe that Paul was an inspired writer, someone who had a mystical relationship to the Risen Christ. But I also believe that he was limited in countless ways and that his views cannot be incorporated into our contemporary dialogue on the various themes raised in this volume without a careful and critical reading.

There is an important caveat here, and it is generally articulated by those who believe the biblical texts are the "Words of God." Are we "liberals" just picking and choosing? Are we avoiding uncomfortable teachings because they speak prophetically to our own vulnerabilities? Or are we really rejecting some of Paul's views because of Paul's own human limitations and his own biases?

These are important challenges to the way of reading the texts that I am following. All that I or any author can do is try to keep these questions always in mind. I find myself compelled to believe that there is a middle way between slavishly believing everything Paul says and arbitarily cherry-picking only those things that appeal to me. This is the challenge to every scholar approaching a text with the tools of a historical-critical method.

The Selection of Texts

Ancient people had a different attitude toward authorship and copyright than we do. Writing anonymously in the name of a great teacher was intended to amplify the teacher's "school of thought," not to be, as we would think of it, a forgery. The entire Torah is attributed to Moses (including the account of his own death!); all the Psalms to David (even Psalm 137, which was written after the Babylonian destruction of the Temple that David didn't live long enough to see built); all the Wisdom literature to Solomon. None of these attributions is literally accurate, yet they serve an important function by symbolically identifying the material with a common source, even if the hands that composed it were different.

In much the same way, a whole body of material in the Christian Testament (as well as a number of writings outside it) are attributed to Paul. Historical and critical textual study has led to a consensus of scholars that seven of the fourteen letters have the highest probability of containing Paul's authentic voice: Romans, 1 Corinthians, 2 Corinthians, Galatians, 1 Thessalonians, Philemon, and Philippians. The criteria used include vocabulary (like any writer, Paul had favorite words), writing style, and historical context.

My investigation of Paul will be restricted to these seven letters. I do not, however, use any of these letters in their entirety. I have chosen passages relating to some of the themes that I see as central to an integrated understanding of Paul's thought. These themes form the ten chapter headings for this study: Paul on Paul; Sin and Grace; Old and New Creation; The Call to Community; The Lord's Supper; Jews and Christians; Teachings on

Sexuality; Love; The End Times; and God's Plan for the Jews. My hope is that in reflecting on these excerpts from the Pauline corpus, the reader will come to know the major issues exercising this religious genius and that they will also help inform our personal efforts for spiritual growth today.

Some of the best-known and even beloved passages from Paul's letters may be missing from this collection. I apologize for that, but my intention is to highlight the central themes of Paul's thinking as succinctly as possible. I hope the passages included will provide a genuine connection to Paul and his thinking, however you have come to regard him, as well as an interesting starting place for your own investigation into the rest of Paul's writing. Let's now consider these ten topics briefly.

PAUL ON PAUL

Although Paul's letters do not contain a great deal of autobiographical material, he does speak of the revelations so central to his sense of identity and mission. His words suggest that he received more than one such revelation. The pattern seems similar to the experience of Muhammad, who received his first revelation in 610 C.E., when he was about forty years old, and continued to receive revelations until his death in 632 C.E. There is every reason to believe that Paul's revelational experiences accompanied him on his life's journey, from his initiating revelation in 33 C.E. to whatever final revelations guided him during his last days on earth.

Another experience shared by Paul and Muhammad is a journey by which each was taken up through the levels of heaven to experience a deep sense of union with God. Today we might understand these levels of heaven as levels of consciousness. One useful tool for teasing out a richer portrait of Paul is to consider the levels of consciousness through which his writings range.

There are many maps of consciousness; some have seven stages, and one has thirteen. I work with a four-layer model of consciousness, comparing it to a house with a basement, a first and second floor, and a roof deck. None of these levels is "bad," and each is appropriate at certain times.

The basement level of consciousness is a tribal consciousness. This is a survival level. We hear a window being broken and run to the basement—actually and metaphorically—to hide in our panic room. This is a black/white way of seeing the world: good guys and bad guys; us and them.

The first floor represents rational consciousness. Here people can live with others who disagree with them. Civil discourse can be enjoyed and creative disagreement and dialogue encouraged. For example, a visitor to this country told me that Americans are probably unappreciative of the simple fact that after election day everyone gets up and goes to work. We don't hide in our basements waiting for a bloody coup staged by the losing candidate.

The second floor represents psychic consciousness. At this level, we begin to intuit a world beyond our plans. There's a Jewish proverb that captures this nicely: "What makes God laugh? Our plans." We are open to intuitions and can read the language of dreams. We can let go of an obsessive need to control our lives and in some sense watch our lives unfold.

Finally, there is the deck on the roof, mystical consciousness. This is a unity consciousness transcending all duality. For the mystics, there can be nothing other than God, though there is a difference between the unmanifest and the manifest Godhead. For example, we can consider a wave in its unique configuration, or from the perspective from which it is nothing more than water. So, too, all of reality is a rhythm of wave and water. As waves, we are many; as water, we are one. This experience of overcoming all dualisms leads to bliss, compassion, and a deep and abiding peace.

The circumstances of life are much the same for folks who hang out mainly in the basement and for those who spend most of their time on the roof deck. What makes our lives different in the long run has nothing to do with circumstances. The difference lies in how we understand and judge those circumstances—that is, in our consciousness.

An awareness of levels of consciousness is extremely important for reading sacred texts. Generally, they contain something for every level of consciousness, but the highest levels can be understood only from the rooftop. In earlier books, I have stated that Jesus's admonitions to put our lights on lampstands (Matt. 5:15) and to proclaim from the housetops what we hear whispered (Matt. 10:27) may be references to levels of consciousness. Our deeds and words will be more powerful when raised to a higher level of consciousness.

The highest teachings can only be understood at the mystical level. Take Jesus's teaching that we are to love our enemies (Matt. 5:44). At the tribal level, such a teaching makes no sense. Enemies are those we hate. At the rational level, we might negotiate with our enemies. At the psychic level, we might begin to feel things from their side. But it is only at the mystical level that we can really love our enemies, since loving the enemy means not having an enemy, not seeing the world in terms of the dualistic mind-set of enemy and friend.

Part of the complexity of Paul consists in the way he moved between levels of consciousness. At times he talked as though there were something punitive in God's nature, clearly a tribal sentiment. At other times, he soared with the mystics, experiencing oneness with God. His autobiographical statements give us hints of this range of consciousness that he, like most of us, experienced. It is not atypical for people to roam through their house of consciousness. Where we spend most of our time, however, has significance and speaks potently to the kind of people we are.

What we don't find in Paul's autobiographical reflections, of course, is any information about his human reality. What were his parents' names? Did he enjoy dining out as much as Jesus did? Did he appreciate the gorgeous sweeps of nature he saw on an almost daily basis? These things we will never know, and he would be surprised by our curiosity to know things of such unimportance. It is nonetheless important for us to begin our study of Paul with whatever autobiographical data we can find, which is the purpose of our explorations in the first chapter.

Sin and Grace

Every spiritual tradition knows about sins—times we miss the mark, fail to love as we should, act without skill, live at a level of consciousness below what is appropriate in a given situation. An example of this is a college student who is short on money stealing twenty dollars from his roommate. As we grow up, it is only natural that we sometimes make mistakes. Goethe wrote: *Es irrt der Mensch solang er strebt.* People will make mistakes as long as they are striving to grow, as long as they are truly living and making conscious choices.

Paul is very concerned about sins, but more than that, he is concerned about Sin with a capital *S*, which he conceives of as a kind of corporate obstacle, like a cloud blocking the light of the sun from everyone who lives beneath it. And for Paul, everyone does live beneath it—the entire human race. We can't change this reality of Sin any more than we can remove the clouds on a dark day.

But what is Sin, exactly? It is not an act but a state of being, something Augustine called *peccatum originale*, original sin. Paul is generally thought to be at the source of this theological tradition, the notion that we are dominated by a sinful condition so overwhelming that in the face of it we are without power or freedom. Even if we steadfastly resist committing sins in our everyday lives, our very condition before God is defined by this ontological reality about which we can do nothing. Hence, our help must come from outside ourselves, and this is the real purpose of Jesus's mission and the true meaning of his death: as an atoning sacrifice for Sin.

What's more, our understanding of sins and Sin determines our understanding of grace, which can be thought of as God's gift-giving character. If Sin is a tragic, aberrant rupture in our very being that we are powerless to overcome, then we do need grace and salvation from outside ourselves, from God. But if our sins result from the normal path of learning to grow up spiritually, then grace is the invitation and power to grow and be transformed. In both cases, God is involved; in the former model, God comes in from outside to fix something wrong in us, whereas in the latter model, God is within us, inviting us to keep on growing.

There is resistance to the theological construct of Sin as a condition of human helplessness in much of contemporary Christian theology. And yet, this seems so central in the message of Paul. We are all dominated by this Sin, and we can't do anything about it. So help must come from somewhere else, from some source totally beyond our choices and decision making. Consequently, only those people who have access to the outside help that Christians have can be saved.

The problem is that this mode of Paul's theology does not seem to be present in the teachings of Jesus. Jesus dealt with Roman officers and sent them home as pagans. He seemed to feel no compulsion to have them wait around until after his death and resurrection, when they could receive the sacrament of baptism and be saved.

Jesus's message seems to encourage an openness to the presence of God that is already growing in all of us because we are made in God's image and likeness. Paul, however, sees us as spiritually bankrupt, needing to be rescued. Many contemporary theologians find it intuitively wrongheaded to imagine that our growth comes from an outside agent instead of through personal spiritual evolution. So when we read Paul, we might have to adjust our sights, realizing that he was gripped by a worldview shared neither by Jesus nor by most of us today.

How we understand the human condition and how we envisage what is required for its healing and wholeness is absolutely fundamental for developing either a theology or a spiritual practice. This question, then, will be the primary focus of our attention in the second chapter.

OLD AND NEW CREATION

The theologian Matthew Fox was the first to make the distinction between Christ as Redeemer and Christ as Reminder. How we understand ourselves in the light of that distinction has a lot to do with how we understand the essential transformation the Christian faith entails. In Colossians 3:9–10 and in Ephesians 4:22–24, Paul, or one of his disciples, urges us to put off the "old self" and put on the "new self." And Paul himself speaks of this essential transformation in numerous other texts. But how is it that we are transformed? Are we "redeemed," or are we "reminded"?

The two words (*redeemer* and *reminder*) succinctly represent two very different ways of understanding the meaning of Jesus's life and death. If we had encountered Jesus on the dusty roads of the Galilee and had asked him about his basic self-understanding, what would he have answered? Would he have said that his purpose was to die for the Sin of the world, to be humankind's redeemer, and that his teaching and healing were just a matter of filling time until that great and climatic moment of his death became a reality? Some Christians who respond to a more Hellenized view of Jesus's mission would say yes.

Other Christians hear a thoroughly Jewish Jesus reply that he recognized in human beings a basic goodness (an original blessing) springing from the divine life that is the deepest dimension of human beings and indeed of all beings, from molecules to mountains. And they further would hear him say that his role was to be a reminder to all he met—the poor and diseased, the wealthy and healthy, the movers and shakers, as well as the marginalized and powerless—that God stands at the door of our lives, waiting only to be invited to enter. And when that door is opened, we indeed become a new creation.

Which model Paul uses in understanding the transition from an old to a new creation will be our central concern in this third chapter.

THE CALL TO COMMUNITY

If there is one area where Jesus and Paul clearly seemed to be on the same page, it is in their understanding of the profound differences between God's reign and Caesar's reign. When Jesus and Paul proclaimed God's reign, they were, in the words of renowned Jesus scholar John Dominic Crossan, in effect, saying: "In your face, Caesar." When Paul asked Christians to say with their lips (in other words, out loud) that Jesus is Lord, this meant that they were not saying what everyone else around them was saying: "Caesar is Lord."

Caesar's reign was founded on four principles, the first of which is that the state is supreme. The emperor is a deity to be worshipped. He is God's son. Second, peace comes through winning wars and military dominance.

The Roman motto was: *Si vis pacem, para bellum.* If you want peace, get ready for war. The much-vaunted Pax Romana (Roman Peace) was achieved through the twenty-six legions patrolling the Roman world. Third, your value lies in your possessions. Historians agree that an insatiable greed was a key contributing factor to the decline of Rome. Fourth, your attitude toward others should be to dominate them. Rome's vocation was to rule.

Just as Caesar's reign had four principles, God's reign had four principles, each subversive to the legitimacy of Caesar's reign. The first principle of God's reign is that God is supreme. Second, peace comes through justice. And justice is fairness: when people perceive themselves to be treated fairly, peace is not far away. Third, your value lies in your relationships. Covenant is perhaps the most important biblical word, and it means to be in relationship. The best life is one of richly textured relationships: with God, with intimate others, with larger communities, with nature itself. Fourth, your attitude toward others should be to serve. This entails empowering others, not having power over them.

Proclaiming God's reign was a threat to Roman power. So it comes as no surprise that both Jesus and Paul were executed as criminals through the judgment of a Roman court. Pontius Pilate was the highest Roman authority in the province Jesus inhabited, and the ancient creed confessed that Jesus suffered "under Pontius Pilate." Paul was judged by a court in Rome. Both were executed as law breakers, as threats to Roman power.

In the passages assigned to this fourth chapter, we will see the way Paul's instructions to his community were intended to help Christians live with one another in a way that was faithful to God's reign.

THE LORD'S SUPPER

The Lord's Supper, also called communion or the Eucharist (from the Greek, meaning "thanksgiving"), is an important rite in Christian tradition that is inspired by the final meal Jesus shared with his disciples on the eve of his arrest. Excommunication means being banned from sharing in the Eucharist, and it has been a powerful weapon in the hands of the Christian church almost from the beginning.

Early councils declared people "anathema" (cursed, rejected, and excommunicated) if they failed to accept certain creedal propositions. Such rejection—even the act of refraining from excommunication—speaks powerfully to the core values of the church in a given time and age. For example, the German bishops decided not to refuse communion to people coming to the altar wearing swastikas. And some American bishops decided to refuse communion to people coming to the altar wearing rainbow banners, signs of support for gay rights.

One of our primary sources on the function and importance of the Lord's Supper is Paul, for whom the community's weekly communion meal was an important topic. From Paul's account and the accounts in three of the four Gospels, there is every reason to believe that Jesus used bread and wine in a final shared meal with his disciples, investing this ritual act with special significance. But there the agreement ends. Exactly what was said and done at that meal has been the source of contention ever since.

Our first account of this meal is in Paul, a text we will examine. His story seems to be the one that was transmitted to Mark and thus to Matthew and Luke. John's Gospel lacked "an institution narrative"—that is, he gave no account of Jesus doing anything with bread and wine, though he presented us with a lengthy account of what Jesus said at that final and fateful meal.

As a graduate student in theology, I took a semester-long course on the theology of the Eucharist, the ceremony of bread and wine, and I often felt drawn to a comment I heard the great twentieth-century German Jesuit theologian Karl Rahner make that, when all is said and done, all we know is that Jesus somehow invested that final meal with great importance.

There are, nevertheless, countless views and opinions about why it is important, or even if it is important. In a visit to the University of Marburg in Germany, I sought out the famous table where Martin Luther, in a debate with other reformers, wrote the Latin words *Hoc est enim corpus meum* (This is my body) on the table and drew a circle around them, telling his fellow reformers that he could not accept a theology that went outside that circle.

Transubstantiation, consubstantiation, commemoration—these are technical terms describing differing views on the nature of the Eucharist. Is Jesus truly present in the elements of bread and wine so that they are no longer bread and wine, except in appearance? Transubstantiation. Is Jesus truly present in the elements of bread and wine, which still remain bread and wine as well? Consubstantiation. Does the union with Jesus reside in the believer's faith rather than in the elements as such? Commemoration.

I remember attending a Protestant service many years ago. I knew the minister and was going home with him for lunch after the service. As he was cleaning up the communion table, I saw him pour the contents of the chalice into a grape juice bottle. I was shocked. It's hard to describe in words how scandalous that was for someone who grew up with the Roman Catholic understanding of communion, where if even one drop from the communion cup was spilled, the whole liturgy stopped while that drop was carefully wiped up with a special cloth that would later be burned and disposed of in no other way. Naturally, I asked my friend what he was doing. He informed me that he was taking it home to drink with his lunch.

How did Paul understand this communion meal? Since Paul's understanding launched all of Christian Eucharistic theology on a particular course, we will examine in this fifth chapter the passages in which he talks about this ritual meal.

JEWS AND CHRISTIANS

When we think of Jews and Christians today, we might imagine a street on which there is a synagogue on one corner and a church on another. It's difficult for us to realize that in Paul's time, the meeting of a Jewish community and the meeting of a Christian community might not have looked all that different. After all, in its origins, the Jesus movement was a Jewish sect.

Some scholars feel that the very language of conversion is inappropriate when applied to Paul, since Paul never converted from one religion to another. He remained a Jew, living according to what he understood to be the correct interpretation of being Jewish. But if Paul's interpretation of "true Judaism" was correct, then his Christian communities (and largely Gentile Christian to boot) represented the "true Israel." Jews who don't agree with Paul are left out in the cold, relegated to having an "Old Testament" and an old and outmoded religion as well.

Alan Race, an Anglican theologian and priest, introduced the concepts of exclusivism, inclusivism, and pluralism into our conversations about other religions. These terms were further made popular by Diana Eck, a Harvard professor and author. They provide an important corrective to what many theologians consider a major limitation in Paul's thought, one that has been inherited by much of the Christian world today, especially by Christian fundamentalists. It consists of Paul's profound inability to affirm a view different from his own. This exclusivism plagued him when he was a Pharisee bent on changing the minds of Jewish Christians, and it continued to plague him as a Jewish Christian bent on changing the minds of Jews and Gentiles alike.

Exclusivism is the belief that my religion has all the truth and that anything outside my religion is error. This attitude characterized Christian attitudes toward other religions for a long time. For example, when Native Americans showed Christian missionaries their sacred sites, the missionaries named all those places after the Devil. So if you are traveling around and see a "Devil's Mountain" or "Devil's Lake," be sure to stop by; it will be a beautiful place. Such missionaries shared Paul's exclusivism and believed that any religion other than theirs was of the Devil. This either/or view of religious allegiance, consonant with tribal or basement consciousness, is alive and well in today's world.

It is arguable that the most common attitude of people of one religion toward people of another is inclusivism. This is the stated position of the Roman Catholic Church in the documents of Vatican II. Essentially, this means that my religion has the fullest articulation of the truth, but your religion may indeed participate in some of that truth.

The inclusivist does indeed include your religion, but only as a deficient form of his own. According to inclusivist Judaism, covenanting with God through the covenant of Sinai is best, but covenanting with God through the covenant of Noah can save you as a non-Jew. According to inclusivist Christianity, all salvation comes through Jesus, but God may find a way to save you as an "anonymous Christian" with no formal faith in Jesus. According to inclusivist Islam, the Qur'an has the fullest and final articulation of true religion, but you, as a Jew or a Christian, can merit paradise by following your respective revelations, though they have been distorted in the course of history.

Pluralism is relatively rare. It is not so much a belief as a hypothesis. It entails regarding another religion in its own integrity, not in comparison to one's own. Just as we don't think of French as inferior Spanish, we would not regard Judaism, for example, as incomplete Christianity. Yet it is quite clear that for Paul, Jews were indeed incomplete unless they accepted his messianic faith. Christian pluralists who feel obliged to carry Paul's ideas forward do so into a context that he, in his own time, would not have understood.

Paul's inability to appreciate dialogue and his deep-set exclusivism are areas of his thought that many theologians find seriously deficient. Incapable of true dialogue, Paul saw other views as unacceptable alternatives to the truth that only his faith could articulate. A lack of humility seems to characterize this kind of thinking, and Christian arrogance (sometimes called triumphalism) has indeed been a constant thread running through the dark pages of Christian history, including persecutions of those who embrace alternative faiths; crusades and inquisitions; insensitive proselytizing; and even immoral missionizing (such as Christian missionary hospitals refusing medical services to the unbaptized).

We will attempt in this sixth chapter to understand Paul's view of those not sharing his faith, and yet find a way to grow beyond his limitations.

I recently reviewed a book called *Sex Texts from the Bible: Selections Annotated and Explained* (SkyLight Paths). All the major texts in the Bible dealing with sexual matters are examined one by one. This book serves an important purpose because the texts in the Bible dealing with sex are among the most profoundly misunderstood in all of scripture.

That misunderstanding started early in Christianity's development; even in our own day, Christians are frequently out of touch with reality when they talk about sex. This is especially true when celibates attempt to give advice on sexual matters. Ignatius of Loyola, who founded the Society of Jesus (popularly known as the Jesuits), demonstrated extraordinary insight into many aspects of spiritual life. But when he comes to celibacy, his injunction to the members of his community consists of three words: *Sint sicut angeli.* Let them be like the angels. This might be construed as an invitation to innocence, but it can be understood equally well as an invitation to ignorance. This lack of sexual wisdom is certainly a contributing factor to the sex scandals that rock various denominations of the church today. Less dramatically, but perhaps more profoundly, it is also the source of many uninformed, unhealthy, and unhelpful cultural standards upheld by so many today.

A prominent evangelical Christian pastor recently confessed to having had regular meetings with a male prostitute, although he had a wife and family. He apologized to his congregation, stating that he had acted immorally and that he had a "repulsive side" that he had been dealing with all of his adult life. Although I certainly felt sorry for his family, to whom he had lied, I felt sorry for him too. I wanted to tell him that he did not have a repulsive side. He was simply a homosexual. That was his nature, and it was no more repulsive than being left-handed. But he comes from a Christian community that profoundly misreads, mistranslates, and misunderstands the biblical texts regarding certain forms of homogenital behavior.

Most scholars agree that Paul does not provide much help to us on these matters. This is hardly surprising, considering that as a Hellenistic

Jew he had little appreciation for sexual union except as a sign of a higher spiritual reality. Even prostitution was more of a spiritual metaphor for Paul than a real-world phenomena. And as an apocalyptic Jew, expecting the end of the present world order in his lifetime, it certainly made no sense for him to be involved in starting a family.

Yet the Christian conversation about sexual matters must begin with Paul, for Jesus had little to say on the subject, showing considerably more concern about justice. The question facing Christians today is how that conversation is to continue in an enlightened fashion that can meaningfully include all we have come to know on the subject since the time of Paul. This provides the focus for the seventh chapter.

LOVE

We overuse the word *love* in our English language. We can love our mothers, out sweethearts, our country, and chocolate ice cream. The Greeks used three words: *eros, philia,* and *agape.* Eros implied a natural attraction to another person. This was not necessarily erotic in our sense of the word but entailed a natural liking of another person. Often, within a few minutes of meeting someone, you know whether or not you like that person.

Philia was the love of friendship. This implied commitment and mutuality, a cultivated relationship. Obviously, just as we cannot like everyone, we cannot be friends with everyone. We Americans use the word *friend* fairly loosely. Living and studying in Germany, I noticed that Germans are more careful to distinguish a *Bekannter* (an acquaintance) from a *Freund* (friend).

Agape could be extended to everyone. It did not involve emotional attraction, mutuality, or long-term commitment. It entailed an unconditional regard for another with behavior appropriate to the circumstance. In other words, we can love the woman at the checkout counter without asking her out to dinner. A friendly smile and a courteous, respectful attitude suffice in that instance. Thomas Aquinas defined love as *velle bonum alterius,* willing the good of the other, and that seems to hit the nail on the head in three succinct Latin words. Agape was the word preferred by

Paul and the other Christian Testament writers for the kind of love we should show to others.

In a French translation of the Psalms, the word *amour* appears in the phrase we translate into English as, "For his great love is without end." This is an attempt to translate the Hebrew word *chesed*. This characteristic of God is difficult to render in English, but many scholars choose the phrase "covenant-making love." In other words, it is a kind of love, but not what is implied in the French word *amour* or the English word *love*.

Chesed is an initiative-taking on the part of God to establish relationships (covenants) with human beings. A person who embodies this divine quality is a Hasid, a word originally used for someone who was deeply spiritual. Today it refers to Jews who identify with one or another of the ultra-Orthodox groups of Judaism.

One can readily see the similarities between agape and *chesed*. It is probable that a combination of these characteristics formed Paul's idea of love, drawing on both his Jewish and Hellenistic background. It provided the core of Paul's understanding of what binds together a community of Christians. And it is to be extended to the Gentile world as well. In Paul's view, however, only Christians, because of their new life as new creations, could fully understand what it was to live in an agapaic community.

In a world where there is so much confusion about love, Paul's words on this topic merit our attention. It's quite common to hear 1 Corinthians 13 read at a Christian wedding, and I personally never feel that it's too much used. Paul's understanding of love deserves the attention that we will try to give it in the eighth chapter.

THE END TIMES

Paul was an apocalyptic Jew. This means that he anticipated a dramatic end to the present world order within his lifetime. Although scholars of the Christian Testament are far from unanimous on this point, many of them would assert that Jesus was not an apocalyptic Jew and that the apocalyptic verses attributed to Jesus in the Gospels were later accretions, misunderstandings that modified his original message.

But what is the difference between an apocalyptic and a nonapocalyptic Jew? John Dominic Crossan argues that in the Jewish prophetic tradition, God waits for us to act; in the apocalyptic tradition, we wait for God to act. My graduate school mentor, Dr. Manfred Vogel, described the apocalyptic mind-set in one of his lectures as "prophecy losing its nerve." Prophecy in this sense is not about making predictions but about speaking God's Word to a present situation and acting from the perspective of that Word.

Biblical prophecy gets confused with predicting the future because a pronouncement about the present inevitably contains a reference to the future. The prophet calls people to repent (to change their path or change their mind) but also points out that a failure to repent will lead to disaster. It's much like a teacher calling a student in and pointing out that the student needs to be more faithful in attending class, doing homework, and preparing for tests. The teacher wants the student to get with the program and do well. But the teacher will naturally point out that if the student fails to engage the work, an F in the course is an inevitable result. The teacher's purpose is not to predict the F, but to help the student avoid it. It is no less the case with the prophets; they want our repentence, not our failure.

Apocalypse is the Greek word for "revelation," literally, pulling back a curtain or taking off a lid. Knowing the calendar of the end times, the apocalyptic writer can pull back the curtain and allow us to share his secret. All that we need to do is align ourselves with God and God's plan, and we will participate in God's cosmic victory. Oppressed minorities are often drawn to this genre of literature. Realizing that they have little power to change the status quo, they are more than happy to let God step in to effect change.

There is often a vengeful tone in this literature. The faithful group of believers will triumph, and the "bad guys" will be destroyed and sent to hell. And all of this is going to happen very soon. Paul was clearly an apocalyptic writer, expecting Jesus to return in glory within his lifetime (1 Thess. 4:15).

Jesus, on the other hand, avoided apocalyptic language; where it was attributed to him, we may be seeing the words of a later editor. I have elaborated on this thesis both in my book, *The Gospel of Thomas: A Guidebook for Spiritual Practice,* and in my translation and commentary in *The Hidden Gospel of Matthew: Annotated and Explained* (both SkyLight Paths.)

To give just one example of how scholars believe the words of Jesus were misunderstood, let's consider Jesus's call to his fellow Jews to live their covenant with God and not to resist the Romans militarily. If they persisted in that course of violent resistance, he pointed out, then the city and Temple would be destroyed by the Romans.

By the time Matthew's Gospel was written some fifty years later, the Temple had been destroyed and Jesus's warning was directed to the coming end of history. But language about a historical event (the destruction of the Temple) was mixed with end-time language. For example, Jesus exhorted his listeners that, if their disobedience should lead to disaster, they should pray that it not happen on a Sabbath or in winter (Matt. 24:20). But this language is followed by words describing the stars falling from heaven (Matt. 24:29). If the stars were falling from heaven, then it doesn't make much difference whether it was winter or summer, weekday or Sabbath. But if the Romans were invading and you had to flee the city, then those circumstances could make a difference for your survival. So it seems clear that Jesus's words about the future destruction of the city and Temple in the wake of continued violent resistance to Rome have been put into an apocalyptic context foreseeing cosmic destruction. But only the former words came from Jesus; the later verses came from an apocalyptic editor.

Like all the great spiritual teachers, Jesus focused our attention on the present moment, on the here and now, with all its potential for spiritual practice and service to others. According to the Gospel of Mark, Jesus was agnostic about the end-time calendars that are so cherished by some Christians: "But about that day or hour no one knows, neither the angels in heaven, nor the Son, but only the Father" (Mark 13:32).

This important difference between Jesus and Paul had a profound effect both on the development of Christian theology and on Christian spirituality. I sometimes ask my Christian students what they mean when they say in the Lord's Prayer the words "Thy kingdom come." Almost every student asked that question responds that he or she is praying for the end of the world and the last judgment. Why, I ask them, do they want the world to end before they have a chance to graduate from college? What a difference if we understand that petition to mean that we are asking to experience more deeply today the presence of the God who dwells within us, the God who is our own deepest reality.

As a Hellenistic Jew, Paul held a disparaging view of the world, and as an apocalyptic Jew, he anticipated the imminent end of the world—a combination that helps explain why he showed little interest in the here and-now physical realities around him. Jesus, on the other hand, who was neither a Hellenistic Jew nor an apocalyptic Jew, had every reason to find God in the present moment and to serve God there as well.

These options remain alive in our world today. They call for careful consideration. This will be our concern in the ninth chapter.

GOD'S PLAN FOR THE JEWS

This is an area of Paul's thought that is at one level deeply moving and yet at another level deeply confused. It all began when Paul tried to solve a false problem that, in turn, stemmed from his exclusivist thought, which caused him to frame it like this: If he is right in his faith, then everyone not sharing that faith is wrong. But why was it that so many of his own fellow Jews were wrong? They, more than any other group, should be ready and eager to receive their Messiah.

The failure of Jews to convert to Christianity was a thorn in the side of Paul and has remained a source of discomfort and embarrassment for exclusivist-minded Christians throughout history. It has also prompted savage acts of Jew-hatred leading to the death of thousands of Jews guilty of nothing more than living their lives as Jews.

Paul, precisely because he had such great love for his people, needed desperately to find an explanation for the disbelief of his fellow Jews.

And this explanation, to be satisfactory to him, had to include a potentially happy ending.

Believing that the end of the present world order was near, Paul realized that the time was limited to draw people into the community of the saved. He observed that, even as his fellow Jews rejected his message, many of the Gentiles received his good news eagerly. This, he concluded, must be part of God's providence. The disbelief of the Jews made room for Gentile converts.

But Paul loved his fellow Jews too much to leave the situation at that point. He argued that eventually the Jews would become jealous, seeing holiness so manifest in people who were formerly Gentile sinners. And so he believed that, in the end, many of the Jews would move to Paul's faith as well.

It was a beautiful solution, but, of course, it never happened. Conservative Christians argue that it will happen at the end, but the end has simply not yet come. Christians who believe that God will rapture the church, taking to heaven all the true believers, misunderstand the text on which that belief is based. This is something we will examine in the body of the text. But this misunderstanding of the text leads them to believe that God's purposes, after the Rapture has taken place, from then on will focus on the Jews. In other words, these Christians are still trying to predict a future in which Paul's answer will turn out to be right.

A solution to a false problem is a false solution. Jews are not in any trouble. They continue to be invited into a covenant with God through the covenant of Sinai. There is no need to worry that they do not want to become Christians. Once we see the false nature of the problem, the necessity for a solution disappears, along with the many theological attempts to make such a solution plausible.

The theological views that Christians have adopted toward Jews and Judaism have repeatedly led to horrible consequences for Jesus's people. It would be irresponsible to end this book without an examination of a theology that proved to be bad news for Jews and without an exploration of a theology that can be good news for Jews. This will guide our investigations in the tenth and final chapter of this book.

Acknowledgments □

There are always so many people to thank. Mark Ogilbee of SkyLight Paths has been an invaluable partner in this enterprise. From his own deep knowledge of Paul, he has been able to react to everything I have written with profound insight and scholarly depth. Responding to his questions and comments has made this book much better than it would otherwise have been. Numerous student workers from Lake Forest College have labored on this project over the years. Bret Nelson and Rich Lopez are the two who have worked most intensively with me in the last stage of this book, and they deserve special mention and thanks. My son Jim, and my daughter Carrie and her husband, Matt, provide a context of joy and peace in my life that always helps my thoughts flow more readily. To all of those I have named and to the many unnamed supporters of my life and work: Thank you.

A Note on the Translation ☐

Translating texts has long been a part of my scholarly work. I was blessed with a Jesuit education where Latin and Greek were part of our high school curriculum. Translations of sermons by Meister Eckhart, letters of Hildegard of Bingen, essays of Franz Rosenzweig, and Matthew's Gospel precede this present work. In all these translations, I reach beyond the literal text to try to make the reader a contemporary of the translated author.

As in my translation of Matthew's Gospel, I attempt in this book to help the reader relate to the Jewish context of the text. *Jesus* is *Jeshu* (Yay-shoo); *Christ* is *Messiah*; *Law* is *Torah*; *James* is *Jacob*, and so forth. I try to avoid words no longer in common use. *Apostle* becomes *ambassador*, and *righteousness* becomes *God-centeredness*. As you read this translation, I want you to feel—to the extent to which this is possible—that you are reading a letter written yesterday, rather than two thousand years ago. I take liberties with the literal Greek text to foster this illusion of contemporaneity, but I strive diligently to do so without changing the basic meaning of the text.

In the biblical passages, I translate the Greek word for "father," when referring to God, as "Parent." My intention is to be inclusive of all the attributes of God, which include both masculine and feminine qualities. In my annotations, however, I use the traditional Christian designation "he" when referring to God to avoid awkward gender-obscuring constructions. This is for convenience only; I am in no way implying that God is a man, male, or even primarily masculine.

Paul on Paul

1 Paul wanted the Galatians to know that he was sent by God, not human beings. Later in this same chapter he wrote: "I want you to know, my brothers and sisters, that the good news announced by me does not come from human beings. I neither received it nor was taught it by any human source. I received it through a revelation of Jeshu the Messiah" (Gal. 1:11–12). Paul did not believe that his calling needed legitimation by those who knew Jeshu in his earthly career. The disciples' superiority in their earthly knowledge of Jeshu meant little to Paul; he and they were made equals by the fact that they all had encountered the Risen Christ.

2 "Christ died for our sins" has become a Christian mantra, but its linguistic simplicity belies its theological complexity. Countless Christians use the words, but this in no way implies their agreement on what Paul meant when he first wrote or dictated them. Noting only the importance of this confessional statement at this point in our inquiry, we will try to unpack its possible meanings in our further exploration of Paul's thoughts.

☐ Sent by God, Not by Human Authorities

I, Paul, am an ambassador, but one sent neither from nor by human beings.[1] I have been sent by Jeshu the Messiah and by God our heavenly Parent, who raised Jeshu from the dead, and by all the members of the Christian community who are with me. I greet all the communities of Galatia with grace and peace from God our heavenly Parent and from the Lord Jeshu, the Messiah, who gave himself for our sins to rescue us from this present evil age, by the will of the God who is our true Parent.[2] May God be praised through all the ages. Amen.

—GALATIANS 1:1–5

1 Tracing this decision to go to Jerusalem to a revelation suggests that there was not simply Paul's inaugural revelation on the road to Damascus, to which so much attention is paid, but a series of revelations on various occasions.

2 The distinction between Jews and Gentiles can also be expressed as a distinction between the circumcised and the uncircumcised. One of Paul's most innovative teachings was that Gentile converts to Christianity should be bound by the moral commandments but not by the holiness codes.

The moral commandments expand on the Golden Rule found in virtually all of the world's spiritual traditions. Obeying the moral commandments (don't steal, for example) is a way of loving others; violating them hurts others. But not being circumcised or violating the dietary laws does no harm to others, though these transgressions of the holiness codes may hurt community identity. Titus was not required to fulfill one of the holiness codes, and Paul considered this a real victory for his viewpoint.

3 The Judaizers, Christians who disagreed with Paul precisely on this point of exempting Gentile converts from the observation of the holiness codes, were constantly opposing Paul's mission. They wanted all converts to Christianity to first become full Jews. Paul saw this view as espousing a kind of slavery.

4 Paul's words show him to be conflicted in his relationship to the Jerusalem authorities, the men who lived with Jeshu during his years of teaching. On the one hand, Paul needed their "right hand of fellowship" as a testimony to their approbation of his mission. On the other hand, he seemed reluctant to admit that he should need their approval, since his commission came directly from revelation. Later events made it clear that not all the members of the Jerusalem community were comfortable with Paul's message and with the type of Christian communities he was establishing. It reminds us of the need to balance Christian unity today with the recognition of a diversity of beliefs among Christians.

5 As mentioned in the introduction, I use the Hebew forms of the names of ambassadors, including James (Jacob), Peter (Rock), and John (Jochanan).

4

☐ Called for the Gentiles

I went to Jerusalem again fourteen years later, accompanied by Barnabas and Titus. I made this trip because of a revelation.[1] I met privately with some of the members of the community there and let them know about the good news that I was announcing to the Gentiles. I did this to make sure that I was not running at cross-purposes with them. Even though Titus was a Gentile Christian, he was not forced to be circumcised.[2] There were some outsiders who slipped into this meeting with the purpose of spying on our freedom in Jeshu the Messiah and trying to push us back into slavery, but we didn't give in to them because we wanted the truth of our good news always to remain with you.[3] Nothing was added to my message or mission by the so-called leaders (what they actually are only God knows, for God is no respecter of titles).[4] It was clear that I had been given a good news for the uncircumcised just as Rock had been given a good news for the circumcised. For the God who worked through Rock making him an ambassador to the Jews also worked through me in my mission to the Gentiles. When Jacob, Rock, and Jochanan (the acknowledged pillars of the community) recognized the grace given to me, they extended the right hand of fellowship to Barnabas and myself.[5] We all agreed that we should go to the Gentiles and they would go to the Jews.

—GALATIANS 2:1–9

1 The Messiah's death for our sins, as well as his burial and his resurrection, were central to Paul's message. How could Paul assert that this was written in scripture? He may have had in mind the enigmatic Suffering Servant talked about in Isaiah 53:5—"He was wounded for our transgressions, crushed for our inequities; upon him was the punishment that made us whole, and by his bruises we are healed." This is probably the clearest passage in the Hebrew Bible in which we can see a theology of vicarious suffering, one person's suffering having a salutary effect on another person or group of people.

2 How is being buried and raised up on the third day also written in scripture? Paul might have been thinking of the verse in Hosea 6:2—"After two days he will revive us; on the third day he will raise us up, that we may live in God's presence." This use of a scriptural passage as an allusion to and an interpretation of an event not part of the text's immediate context belongs to a type of Jewish commentary tradition called midrash.

3 Paul's account of resurrection appearances suggests mystical rather than physical manifestations. For Paul listed his own experience of the Risen Messiah as no different from the others. And yet, Paul never claimed to touch the Messiah's body, as Thomas did in John 20:27, or shared with him a breakfast at the beach, as the other disciples did in John 21:12. This earliest testimony to resurrection appearances seems to point to individual or shared mystical experiences, not to bodily manifestations in the physical realm.

☐ Paul as Witness of the Risen Messiah

What I passed on to you as most important is what had been passed on to me—namely, that the Messiah died for our sins as it is written.[1] He was buried and then raised on the third day, also as it is written.[2] He appeared to Rock, then to the Twelve, then at one time to five hundred members of our community. Most of them are still alive, though some have passed on. The Messiah then appeared to Jacob and then to all the ambassadors. Finally he appeared to me, a baby prematurely born. For I am the least of the ambassadors, not fit even to be called an ambassador, since I was once actively persecuting God's people.[3] But by God's grace I am what I am, and that grace has not been without results. I can even claim that I am working harder than any of the other ambassadors, though it's God's grace working in me and not the efforts of my own ego.

—1 CORINTHIANS 15:3–10

1 The text talks of Hebrews and Israelites, but there were neither Hebrews (the people leaving Egypt under Moses) nor Israelites (the inhabitants of the ancient Jewish kingdoms) at the time of Paul. These are references to the past, as though an American were to say: "If they came over on the Mayflower, so did I."

2 Paul expressed some hesitancy about bragging so shamelessly. Otherwise, he wouldn't have called it foolishness and craziness. But it was not uncommon for Paul to feel a need to defend himself against his critics. After all, he didn't have the credentials of those who shared in Jeshu's Galilean ministry. On the other hand, some of the passages we explore in chapter 1 indicate quite clearly that Paul never considered himself inferior to those who did hold such credentials. Paul argued that his ministry had sufficient credentials through the personal revelations granted to him.

It is also quite possible, of course, that Paul's expressed diffidence about bragging was a rhetorical device and that he did indeed feel the need to do this for the sake of the often testy members of the community at Corinth. Paul experienced numerous difficulties with this community, and his authority was frequently challenged there. Perhaps he considered it of crucial importance that the Corinthians know something of the dangers that accompanied his missionary activity.

3 There is probably little hyperbole in Paul's list of hardships. Travel in the ancient world was fraught with all the dangers Paul listed. I have visited some of the cities in Turkey where Paul stayed. The sheer distances Paul covered impressed me, especially when I imagined covering all those miles by foot. The terrain was rugged and rocky, not readily conducive to walking. And who knows what kind of shelter awaited Paul at the end of the day?

☐ Paul's Dangerous Mission

If anyone has the nerve to brag—and I realize it's foolishness—so do I. Are they descendants of the ancient Hebrews? ... me too. Are they descendants of the citizens of the former kingdom of Israel? ... me too.[1] Are they in the service of the Messiah? If you can indulge a little more of my craziness,[2] me too, only more so: more struggles, more jail time, more floggings, more life-threatening situations. On five occasions I received from the Jews the punishment of thirty-nine lashes. On three occasions I was beaten with rods. Once stones were thrown at me. I was shipwrecked three times, adrift at sea for a night and a day, constantly on the road, dealing with dangerous rivers, dangerous bandits, dangerous Jews, dangerous Gentiles, urban dangers, rural dangers, maritime dangers, dangers from people falsely claiming to be brothers and sisters. I have lived long with labor and hardship; I have endured a lot of sleepless nights, hungry and thirsty, with no prospect of food, cold and naked.[3] And in addition to everything else, I have the daily pressure of trying to take care of all the Christian communities.

—2 CORINTHIANS 11:21–28

1 Wisdom is an important theme in biblical literature. The Hebrew word means "skill," so that playing a flute or expertly baking bread would be a form of wisdom. Some of the wisdom teachings are like recipes, practical methods for finding success in the workplace, for dealing with spouses, for rearing children. Yet there are other genres of wisdom teachings that touch on more profound mysteries, including evil and suffering and the meaning of life itself.

2 Worldly wisdom, or the wisdom of politicians, is based on the premises of Caesar's reign: the state is supreme; peace comes from military conquest; possessions are the important thing in life; and one's attitude toward others should be based on the will to dominate. This stands in total contrast to God's reign as Jeshu proclaimed it and as Paul understood it.

Caesar's reign and those who live their lives loyal to it end up destroying everything that makes life most meaningful. Like King Midas turning everything to gold, including his own daughter, Caesar's reign turns everything into profit and power, missing the mystery completely.

3 God's wisdom, the wisdom Paul was willing to share with those who were spiritually mature, is of a totally different kind. It will inevitably be understood as foolishness by those who accept the premises of Caesar's reign, because God's wisdom is based on the premises of God's reign: God is supreme; peace comes from justice; our relationships are our most valuable possessions; our attitude toward others should be a desire to serve. This is the source of true greatness, the goal that all the sacred traditions teach, but it can only be understood by those who have embarked on a path of spiritual growth. Paul urged the members of his community to walk courageously on this path, one that is no less relevant to our time than to his.

☐ Paul Announces God's Wisdom

When I'm with those who are spiritually mature, I do talk about wisdom.[1] But this is not a worldly wisdom, a wisdom that our political leaders could understand; their kind of wisdom is leading them to destruction.[2] I talk about God's wisdom, something secret and hidden, something God disclosed from all eternity for our glory.[3]

—1 CORINTHIANS 2:6–7

1 Paul believed that his mission and message were from God, mediated by God's direct revelation. That's why Paul's confidence was rooted in God and not in his own talents or virtues.

2 Paul saw himself called to proclaim a new covenant, a new way for humankind to be in a relationship with God. This covenant was not based on the fleshy rituals described in the Hebrew Bible, such as circumcision and animal sacrifice. All of these ancient practices were closed to the Spirit. Paul believed that they were but pale allusions to what had finally arrived in the covenant mediated by Jeshu the Messiah.

We see Paul's Hellenistic mind-set here. He saw a clear dichotomy between death-producing Flesh and life-giving Spirit. Flesh does not mean merely what is physical or bodily, although Paul occasionally used it that way. After all, baptism and communion were physical and bodily as well. But for Paul these rituals were not fleshly; they were not caught at the lower realm of reality connoted by Flesh. For Paul, Judaism without faith in Jeshu the Messiah was ineluctably in the Flesh, and that was why it could never mediate the Spirit.

Paul saw the literal and the fleshly as identical. They were no more than two ways of describing being stuck in the nonspiritual realm. Paul's clear teaching was that only faith in Jeshu the Messiah could take the whole of the old covenant and elevate it from the realm of Flesh to that of Spirit.

☐ Paul as Minister of a New Covenant

It is through the Messiah that we have confidence before God.[1] This confidence doesn't rest on anything stemming from us. It comes from the God who enabled us to be ministers of a new covenant, one understood spiritually, not literally, for what is literal kills but what is spiritual gives life.[2]

—2 CORINTHIANS 3:4–6

1 Once again, Paul seemed torn between his need to testify about some of his extraordinary experiences and his fear that he would seem to others to be bragging. Speaking about his own experiences as though they were someone else's seems disingenuous and unhelpful, though in Paul's circles this may well have passed as modesty. The commentators are fairly unanimous on the point that it makes no sense for Paul to be talking about another person here.

2 The idea of heavenly levels was common to the mystical vocabulary of that time. Paul demonstrated some sophistication in these matters by his awareness that such experiences could be in or outside the body. Later mystics, including Teresa of Avila, followed Paul in this kind of precision. An experience in the body would suggest a bodily translation to the heavenly realm; an experience outside the body would be at a mystical level in which no change of location was involved.

3 One wonders why a secret would be revealed that should not be further imparted. It would not in that case relate to Paul's mission and message but to something pertaining entirely to his own interior life, something for his own personal enrichment.

4 There has been much speculation concerning the nature of this "thorn in the flesh." Whatever the nature of this thorn, it is important to understand how it functioned in Paul's life. Even though it was understood as satanic in its origin, this problem—whatever its nature—played a role in Paul's spiritual life. Neither Paul nor any of us is expected to be without shadow or fault. The best healers are wounded healers. Our shadow, when properly understood, enhances the figure cast by our light. The truest kind of power is aware of its weakness.

☐ Paul as Recipient of Divine Revelations

Although I know nothing is gained by it, it's necessary for me to brag about some visions and revelations from the Lord.[1] I know someone in the Messiah who fourteen years ago was taken up to the third heaven—whether this was an experience in or outside the body I don't know.[2] And I further know that this person—again I don't know whether this experience was in or outside the body—was taken up into paradise where he heard secrets that no human being should repeat.[3] I'll brag about someone like this, but as for myself, I have nothing to brag about but my weakness. And yet, if I want to brag, I'm no fool, because I'd be telling the truth. But I hold back from this kind of bragging so that people don't think I'm anything more than what they see and hear when they meet me, even though these revelations are quite extraordinary. To keep me from being too proud, I was given a thorn in the flesh, a messenger of Satan to give me grief and keep me from being too proud. On three occasions I asked the Lord about taking this away, but the Lord assured me: "My grace is enough for you, for it's only in weakness that power can reach its fullness." So now I'm willing and happy to brag of my weaknesses so that the Messiah's power can live in that weakness. So I'm perfectly happy with weaknesses, insults, hard times, persecutions, and disasters for the Messiah's sake; for it's only when I am weak that I am strong.[4]

—2 CORINTHIANS 12:1–10

Sin and Grace

1 I capitalize *Sin* to distinguish it from the sins that virtually all sacred traditions recognize. As beings of Flesh (with a capital *F*), we are slaves of Sin. But Flesh is not this envelope of skin we have but a whole level of being and operating that is lower than Spirit. If Paul considered human beings doomed to inhabit the realm of Flesh unless rescued by an outside agency, then Paul did indeed invent original sin as it is most commonly understood among Christians today.

2 Paul's conflicted nature was highlighted in these words. This has led scholars to pursue the source of that conflict. Did Paul, for example, feel a homosexual orientation that he found himself helpless to change? Did he perhaps suffer from a chemical imbalance leading to states of mind over which he had no control? We will probably never know. What we do know, however, is that Paul's self-denigration has become part and parcel of his legacy to Christian thought.

3 This sentence tells us that whatever Paul despised in himself was despised in the Torah as well. And yet, he felt impotent to initiate change. Paul's problem is not an uncommon one. We may know something is bad and yet find ourselves unable to avoid doing it. A person in the first stages of emphysema knows that smoking cigarettes can only exacerbate his condition but may nonetheless find himself unable to kick the habit.

4 Paul's conflicted state was so intense that he finally denied ownership of his actions. It was Sin that must be doing these things in Paul. It is not uncommon for people to disassociate from what they find unacceptable in themselves by attributing it to something or someone else: "The Devil made me do it."

Nevertheless, this kind of victimhood is regarded today by most students of human behavior as immature. The shadow needs to be acknowledged, owned, and even embraced if growth is to occur. Otherwise, one remains at a magical level of operating, trying to conjure up an external power to effect what can be achieved only by oneself. Pauline scholarship has not been hesitant to ask whether certain Christian doctrines may in fact be rooted in Paul's personal, psychological limitations.

☐ Did Paul Invent Original Sin?

We know that the Torah is spiritual, but I am fleshly, a slave sold to Sin.[1] I don't really understand what I'm doing. I end up not doing the things I want to do and doing the things I despise.[2] By doing the things I despise, I'm recognizing that the Torah is good.[3] But I'm really not the one doing these things; rather, it's Sin that is my inner principle of action. For I realize that nothing good inhabits me insofar as I am Flesh. I can want to do what is right, but I'm not capable of doing it. I'm not doing the things I want to do, and I'm doing the things I despise. But if I'm doing things I despise, then it can't really be me that's doing these things but Sin inhabiting me.[4]

—ROMANS 7:14–20

1 Theological language often generates its own problems. If you tell someone, "No matter how great your sin, God's grace is greater," then the person hearing you might conclude that he or she can sin carelessly because God's grace will always be greater. This kind of thinking misses the point. Paul was encouraging us to trust the future God offers us, a future that always transcends the past, including its failures. But to sin recklessly or even deliberately would clearly be an example of "testing the Lord," hardly the response Paul expected.

2 Paul was suspicious of acts like circumcision, rightly recognizing that a person's life may not correspond to the covenant symbolized by the act. Why was Paul not similarly suspicious of baptism? Just because someone had been immersed in water, could Paul presume that the person had been totally transformed? Paul viewed baptism as a spiritual and mystical reality, while relegating physical circumcision to the realm of Flesh.

3 Going down into the water and then emerging from it symbolizes a passage from death to life. Baptized Christians are called to realize that they have symbolically killed the "old self" (their ego-centered identity), emerging as a "new self" (a God-centered identity). Many theologians today would consider this a promise and a commitment, not something that happens by some kind of magic.

Would Paul agree? Would he acknowledge that spiritual growth is accomplished step by step, like any other growth? That the mystery of baptism challenges the Christian to a day-by-day assimilation of the symbolized transition from an ego-centered to a God-centered existence?

□ What Paul Means by Sin and Grace

What do you expect me to say? Should we keep on sinning so that God's grace can increase? That makes no sense. We have died to Sin so how can we keep on living in it?[1] Don't you know that our baptism into Jeshu the Messiah was a baptism into his death?[2] So by baptism into his death, we have been buried with him. And this is so that we can walk in new life, just as the Messiah was raised from death by the Father's glory. After all, if we're one with him in death, we'll certainly be one with him in risen life. It was our old self that was put on the cross with him so that the body of Sin could be destroyed and we would no longer be slaves to Sin. For whoever has died is freed from Sin.[3]

—ROMANS 6:1–7

1 Throughout this passage, Sin—the ontological condition of separation from God—is used in the singular to distinguish it from sins, the everyday failings we all experience. This usage of Sin suggests not individual acts (sins), but a condition causing us to miss the goal of God-centeredness. The consensus of scholars is that Paul understood this, not as a tendency (as in Judaism), but as a compulsion (as in classical Christian doctrine).

2 The image of handing our bodies over to Sin is striking. It seems to imply some degree of freedom. But we need to keep in mind that Paul was writing to baptized Christians. Would the nonbaptized have enjoyed such freedom? Presumably not. In that case, Paul was certainly paving the road to a later model of theological understanding that took for granted human depravity, predestination, and an exclusivist claim to God's grace.

3 Paul exhorted his listeners to hand themselves over to God and specifically to hand their bodies over to God. This implied freedom, but we notice that the source of that freedom lay in having been returned from death to life. The old, sin-bound person died and what rose with Christ was a new creation. This new creation had the capability, as well as the responsibility, to choose God. And that in turn meant living by grace, living with the awareness that all was a gift.

4 Paul argued that to live by grace is to be aware of the gift, whereas to live by the Torah implied a dependence on works, things over which we have control, such as being circumcised or not eating pork.

The distinction seems too facile. Why choose between grace and Torah when a Torah-centered life can be lived gracefully? There is a real distinction between faith-works and law-works, between trusting in works to win God's grace and trusting in God's grace in the performance of works.

But this distinction does not separate Jews and Christians. Both communities have members who trust in God as they perform good works in the world; both communities have members who trust in their good works to merit God's favor and attention.

☐ Who or What Is in Charge?

You shouldn't be subject to your passions by letting Sin control your mortal bodies.[1] You should no longer hand over your bodies to Sin as tools of evil.[2] Hand yourselves over to God, conscious of having been returned from death to life. And hand over your bodies to God as tools of God-centeredness.[3] Sin won't be able to run your lives when you live by grace and not by the Torah.[4]

—ROMANS 6:12–14

1 This whole business of testing is tricky. The same Greek word can mean "test" or "temptation," though the concepts are quite different. I prefer translations of the Lord's Prayer that say "Don't let us fail when we are tested" rather than "Lead us not into temptation."

After all, in the Letter of James 1:13, we read that "God himself tempts no one." In our English usage, tempting often involves trying to trick or deceive someone, but testing is straightforward and honest. Teachers test students, and life tests us all.

2 This assertion of God's faithfulness conveys an important message for the spiritual life of all of us. Testing is intrinsic to growth, and God will certainly test us in many ways. But just as a good teacher doesn't ask a question on a test that the student has not had the background material to handle, so too God does not test us without knowing that we have the resources to grow through the particular challenge with which we are faced. This can be a great source of consolation in the struggle to grow spiritually.

☐ Paul Explains the Ways God Tests People

If you think you're solid on your feet, watch out that you don't slip.
You've not been tested in any way that others haven't been tested too.[1]
God is faithful and won't let you be tested beyond what you can handle.
In whatever way God tests you, you'll be provided with the way to deal
with that test so that you'll be able to handle it.[2]

—1 Corinthians 10:12–13

1 The idea of anyone or anything provoking God's wrath is foreign to much of contemporary Christian theology. We realize today that those who believe that God gets angry and wants to punish people are telling us more about themselves than about God. We know more today about stages of consciousness and the way God is conceived at these various stages. For the tribal person, God is a vengeful warrior. But for the mystic (for example, Julian of Norwich), there is only love in God, nothing punitive, nothing wrathful.

The "wrath of God" Paul speaks of may reflect more of Paul's anger than God's. One can certainly argue that wicked people are not highly evolved spiritually, but is God someone who wants to punish us for not being fully grown up or someone who is with us on our journey to holiness and wholeness?

2 The natural-law argument is that human beings can know God's existence through the works of God. The Qur'an teaches that we can all know God's existence through God's signs. Yet in a suffering and often chaotic world, seeing God shining through creation may not be as easy as Paul seemed to imagine.

3 What was evident to Paul may not be so evident to many of those who have grown up in a challenging world—terrorized by war, brutalized by society, sinned against by those who should have been their caregivers. Paul may have painted with too broad a brush in his assertion that no one could possibly have a valid reason for not knowing about God's existence.

☐ Paul Sees Creation Pointing to the Creator

For the wrath of God is revealed from heaven against every kind of wickedness and lack of God-centeredness among those who trample on the truth through their lack of God-centeredness.[1] For what can be known about God is evident to them because God has made it evident. For even though God's eternal power and divine nature are invisible, they can be understood and seen through all that God has made since the beginning of creation.[2] So no one has a valid reason for not knowing about God's existence.[3]

—ROMANS 1:18–20

1 Paul lived in a world where animal sacrifice was a normal part of religion, something practiced by Jews and non-Jews alike. The annual atonement sacrifice of the Jews was a high point in Jewish cultic practice. It would be perfectly natural for Paul, or any other Jewish Christian at that time, to see Jeshu's bloody death though the lens of the bloody sacrifices at the Temple's altar. The final act of submitting to such a cruel death sealed a life of love and service. All of humankind was somehow healed and elevated by this death that consummated such a God-filled life.

Paul, however, developed this metaphor from premises that many contemporary Christians find difficult to affirm. First, the idea that humankind lay helpless in its sinfulness. Second, the idea that Jeshu's death was the only solution to this problem. Third, the idea that one had to have a conscious connection to this death in order to be released from sin's dominion. Much of contemporary Christian theology suggests alternative starting points.

☐ Paul Separates Sinners and Saved

Everyone is in the same predicament, since all are sinners falling short of God's glory; they are all made God-centered by the gift of God's grace. This comes about through Jeshu the Messiah, who is the redeemer put forward by God as an atonement sacrifice in his blood, made real for us by our faith. God did this to show that God is the true Center. God was willing to put up with all the sins of humankind up to this present time to demonstrate now that God is the Center and that he offers God-centeredness to anyone who has faith in Jeshu.[1]

—ROMANS 3:22B–26

1 Paul made an argument here for the priority of faith over the ritual act of circumcision. No outward sign could be the cause of faith. This represented another take on the central problem of Sin and grace that is the focus of this chapter. How do we get saved, God-centered?

Paul argued that Abraham trusted in God and achieved God-centeredness before he was circumcised, therefore, independent of circumcision. This became an important piece of evidence for Paul because it seemed to negate the importance Jews put on circumcision.

In the example of Abraham, Paul saw a precedent for Gentile Christians being God-centered through faith, without being circumcised. And if Gentile converts didn't need to be circumcised, why would they need to observe any other holiness code?

Paul considered it extremely important to remember that when Abraham was circumcised, it was not his circumcision that made him God-centered. Circumcision was a seal of the God-centeredness he already possessed through faith.

2 Paul concluded that Abraham was the true ancestor both of Jewish and of Gentile Christians. Although the former were circumcised (as was Paul) and the latter were not, that had no bearing on the fact that they both became God-centered through their faith in what God did through Jeshu the Messiah.

Since Paul understood himself to have been called to bring a message to the Gentiles, he was insistent in his belief that Gentile Christians were in no way to be construed as second-class citizens, inferior to their brothers and sisters who were Jewish Christians.

Many scholars consider Jeshu's vision of an egalitarian community of brothers and sisters to be central to Jeshu's teaching. If such is the case, this was certainly an ideal that Paul tried to emulate. Paul's vision of a radically equal Christian community lays a claim on our own spiritual communities today.

☐ Paul Contrasts Faith and Circumcision

We say that Abraham's faith counted as God-centeredness. How did this happen? Was it before or after his circumcision? It was before, not after. He received the sign of circumcision as a seal of the God-centeredness he had by faith while he was still without circumcision.[1] This was all done so that Abraham could be the ancestor both of the uncircumcised who believe, whose faith counts as God-centeredness, and of the circumcised who are not only physically circumcised but also believe, following the faith example of our ancestor Abraham who had faith before being circumcised.[2]

—ROMANS 4:9B–12

1 The acclamation "Caesar is Lord" was the watchword of the Roman Empire. But Paul exhorted Christians to declare aloud "Jeshu is Lord." This entailed a public pledge to dedicate one's life, perhaps even to lose one's life, in loyalty to God's reign. This was a subversive act and played a role in Paul's execution at the hands of the Romans.

Declaring aloud that "Jeshu is Lord" meant recognizing God as supreme, working for justice, developing community, and serving others. There are, of course, many Christians today who understand these words in the privatized context of a personal relationship to Jeshu, not appreciating the total life commitment those words imply.

In Paul's day to declare "Jeshu is Lord" was treason, since it denied the divine nature of the emperor as the lord of all those inhabiting the lands Rome had conquered. In today's world, this declaration may seem treasonable as well. It denies putting national interests above justice. It denies the greed that flies in the face of Jeshu's most basic teachings. It involves those who make this declaration with people in Africa experiencing drought because of environmental destruction, with people in the United States lacking health care, food, housing, or adequate education. These words commit those who declare them out loud to a world-transforming struggle and to unending resistance to the voices of empire.

2 How does this basic Easter faith relate to salvation? The fact that Jeshu the Messiah reigns now with God is a vindication of the earthly message and mission of Jeshu. From the perspective of Caesar's reign, Jeshu died a total failure; it is only from the perspective of faith in God's reign that Jeshu's death can be understood as the victory of risen life.

3 Paul was quoting Isaiah 28:16. The New Revised Standard Version translation is: "One who trusts will not panic."

4 Paul was quoting Joel 2:32. Paul's own life was a testament to the truth that "calling on the Lord" was not a mere matter of words but a recognition that the one you called on as Lord defined the priorities on which your life was built.

☐ Paul Exhorts Christians to Declare Jeshu as Lord

If you declare aloud "Jeshu is Lord"**1** and believe in your heart that God has raised him from the dead, you will be saved.**2** For it is by heartfelt faith that we become God-centered and by public affirmation that we are saved. We read in the scriptures that no one who believes in God will be put to shame.**3** No distinction is made between Jew and Gentile. The same Lord is Lord of all, generous to all who call on him. For we read in the scriptures that everyone who calls on the name of the Lord will be saved.**4**

—ROMANS 10:9–13

Old and New Creation

1 Paul's Hellenistic mind-set looms large in these first two sentences. How strange not to look at people in their physical reality, especially if we regard their physical reality as integral to their being. Paul was, however, enough of a Platonist to see anyone's physical reality as at best a pale reflection of their spiritual reality. Consequently, he was certainly consistent in not being interested in the Messiah as a physical being.

In extreme forms of Hellenistic thought, the physical is inherently evil. As a Jew, however, even a Hellenistic Jew, Paul was certainly aware of the teaching in Genesis that creation is good. This meant that Paul could not go so far as to demonize the physical; but he certainly could and did disparage it. And Christian spirituality has echoed that bias ever since.

This tendency to be dismissive of the physical world is particularly tragic in light of Jeshu's enthusiastic embrace of the physical world— the beauty of the flowers of the field, the joy of sharing good food and wine, the delight in being with children. For Jeshu, the physical world was not at all an obstacle on the way to God; it was the way. How different from Paul, who in all his writings never once described the physical world that he inhabited.

2 There is power in the affirmation of a new creation, a renewal, a re-creation. It is in the experience of Jeshu the Messiah that Christians experience a new birth, a new lease on life, new eyes with which to see the world.

The less than savory corollary to this spiritual re-creation, however, is the exclusivity of Paul's vision, implying that there is no other way in which the new creation can be experienced. One of the challenges to Christianity today is to continue to proclaim its good news without making it bad news for all those who experience the Divine in a different way.

□ The Old Has Vanished

We no longer look at people in their physical reality. Even if we once knew the Messiah in his physical reality, that would no longer be the way we would regard him.[1] Anyone who is with the Messiah is a new creation. Everything old has vanished; now it's all new.[2]

—2 CORINTHIANS 5:16–17

1 From Paul's perspective, did Adam's successors inherit Sin from their common ancestor? Did Paul believe that all people after Adam sinned because they had no other choice? Did he consider human nature so impotent that human beings inevitably lived under the power of Sin? Answering these questions in the affirmative would be the most likely choice for most students of Paul, myself included.

An alternative view—not one shared by Paul, however—would assert that Adam's story is the story of all people to the extent that we all make mistakes in learning to grow up. Nothing compels us to miss the mark; no power of Sin dominates us. Nothing in our nature is intrinsically evil. But in the process of growing from good to better, we will inevitably get it wrong sometimes.

2 Paul claimed that the Torah revealed sins of which we might otherwise have no knowledge. So sin had a different character where the Torah was not known.

3 What exactly did Paul mean by saying that not everyone who followed Adam sinned in the same way that Adam did, but nonetheless sinned? Paul may be implying that Sin (the condition of separation from God) is shared by everyone, but we can differ from one another in the ways in which we sin.

4 Paul hinted at something here that he developed later on in this letter to the Romans. If Adam was quintessentially the human being who disobeyed God, then would there ever be someone who completely and perfectly obeyed God? If so, then Adam, in his very failure, pointed ahead to one who would not fail. Sin and death reign in Adam; grace and life in the Messiah. In the last analysis, we incarnate one of these typologies in our own life, disobedient with Adam or faithful with the Messiah.

☐ Adam as Antitype

Sin came into this world through Adam and as a result of that sin came death, a fate that reached everyone because everyone sinned.[1] Sin, of course, was in the world before the giving of the Torah to Moses, but where the Torah is not known, sin doesn't count in the same way.[2] And yet, death reigned from Adam to Moses, even for those whose sins were not like Adam's.[3] So Adam became an antitype of the one who was to come.[4]

—ROMANS 5:12–14

1 How did Adam's sin cause the reign of death? By beginning a long history or cycle of sin—Cain's murder, the violence of Noah's generation, the pride of Babel's builders? Or by an ontological change in human nature, an idea that later took shape in Augustine's theory of original sin? Probably the latter.

And how is it that people receive grace and God-centeredness through Jeshu? Does it come about through some magical transformation brought about solely by mentally assenting to the efficacy of his atoning death? Or is it through the ritual of baptism? Or is it by using Jeshu as a model for one's own decisions and actions? Many contemporary Christian scholars are drawn to the third option, but it would almost certainly not have been Paul's choice.

2 How did Adam's sin lead to death and condemnation for all human beings? And how does Jeshu's obedience to God lead to life and God-centeredness for all human beings? Paul certainly believed that all human beings were sinners. Did he also believe in universal salvation? Probably not.

Many wonder why Paul didn't clarify these issues further. Perhaps it was because central to Paul's life and thinking was the transformation he experienced; he operated more from an experience of power than from a conceptual framework. Paul was neither a philosopher nor a theologian. He didn't possess that calm rationality we connect with Aristotle, Aquinas, or Immanuel Kant. His brilliant mind moved intuitively, drawing on everything he knew from books and people, from theater and athletic competition, from prayer and personal revelation.

3 How are we made sinners by Adam's disobedience and how are we made God-centered by Jeshu's obedience? Paul's assertion is clear, but his explanation is not. The traditional answer to this question saw Adam's sin as causing an ontological change in human nature, a change that could be reversed only by Jeshu's atoning death.

A different answer to this question sees Adam's sin as a type of the human propensity to miss the mark and sees Jeshu's faithfulness as a model of what we all can be if we open ourselves to God's presence in us.

☐ The Old and New Adam

If it was one man's sin that caused the reign of death, then it's even more certain that those who receive the fullness of grace and the free gift of God-centeredness through the one man, Jeshu the Messiah, will experience the reign of life.[1] For just as one man's sin led to everyone's condemnation, so one man's act of God-centeredness leads to everyone's God-centeredness and life.[2] For even as we were all made sinners by one man's disobedience, so are we all made God-centered by one man's obedience.[3]

—ROMANS 5:17–19

1 In Leviticus 23:9, the Lord, through Moses, commanded the people to bring "the sheaf of the first fruits of your harvest to the priest." The dedication of the first bushel of wheat became a sign that the whole field of wheat was offered to God. Jeshu (like the first fruits) has been taken into the heavenly Temple by being the first to be raised from the dead. Thus, using the first fruits analogy, all those "who belong to him" (those who are, so to speak, part of his harvest) are taken into the heavenly Temple as well.

2 Paul compared Adam and Jeshu, contrasting Adam's disobedience with the obedience of Jeshu. He further contrasted the death that followed Adam's disobedience with the life that followed the obedience of Jeshu.

3 Paul's use of the phrase "those who belong to him" clarifies the preceding verse, which claimed that we will *all* be made alive in the Messiah. Paul's use of *all* must be understood in his exclusivist context. Perhaps he meant that all the readers of his letter or all those with faith will be made alive in the Messiah, but certainly not all of humankind.

Paul was not preaching universal salvation. Paul still clung to a tribal mind-set in which God is sometimes both angry and punitive. Many contemporary Christian scholars offer an alternative view, affirming universal salvation, confident that God could never allow any part of manifested divinity to be separated from the Godself.

4 The passage ends with a mystical vision of the end of human and, indeed, cosmic history. The God who is the source of the Son and all of creation is now the goal to which everything returns. As there was only God in the beginning, so too is there only God in the end.

Here and in numerous other places in his letters, Paul clearly distinguishes Jeshu from God (*theos*). Jeshu comes from the divine realm, according to Paul, and possesses a nature different than our own. But Jeshu is not God and in the end is subordinated to God, along with everything and everyone else. It's somewhat puzzling that the early church councils didn't find Paul's belief a roadblock to the trinitarian dogmas they developed in which Father, Son, and Spirit are equally divine.

☐ The Messiah Goes Before Us

The fact is that the Messiah has been raised from the dead as the first fruits of those who have fallen asleep.[1] Just as death came through a human being, so too has the resurrection of the dead come through a human being. For just as we all die in Adam, so will we all be made alive in the Messiah.[2] But this happens in a certain order: the Messiah as the first fruits, followed by those who belong to him.[3] And at the end, he turns over the reign to God the heavenly Parent. This comes after he has nullified every ruler, every authority, and every power. For it is necessary for him to reign until all of his enemies are subordinate to him. Death is the last enemy to be nullified. For everything is subordinate to his reign; everything, of course, except God, for the Son himself will finally be subordinate to God so that God may be all in all.[4]

—1 CORINTHIANS 15:20–28

The Call
to Community

This powerful admonition contains a whole program for living. It means saying no to the reign of Caesar and yes to the reign of God. It points to the triple transformation inherent in all spiritual practice: a transformation of consciousness, of conscience, and of community.

In the introduction, four levels of consciousness are discussed in connection with chapter 1, Paul on Paul. Spiritual growth necessitates moving from a survival-based, black-and-white consciousness (often called tribal consciousness) through rational and psychic consciousness, to a mystical consciousness, a unity consciousness in which we are concentric with the divine reality, God-centered. This movement is not from bad to good but from good to better.

This change in consciousness will, in turn, lead to a transformation of our conscience, the way we relate to everything outside ourselves through conscious choices. And a transformed consciousness and conscience will inevitably lead to the transformed community that is the goal of Paul's exhortation. Without this triple transformation, a Christian community doesn't look much different than any secular assembly.

The word *teleion* is usually translated as "perfect." But the Greek word contains the root *telos,* which means "goal," "end," or "destination." In other words, it implies something becoming all that it has the capacity to be. The German word for *perfect, vollkommen*, says it all. We are perfect to the extent to which we become full, like the fully opened flower or ripened fruit. In other words, perfection entails our full evolution. There is a progression in the three words Paul chose, a growth from what is good, to what is acceptable to God, to what is fully evolved.

☐ Not Conformity but Transformation

Don't conform yourself to this present world but transform your consciousness so that you will be aligned with God's will, knowing what is good, what is acceptable to God, and what is fully evolved.[1]

—ROMANS 12:2

1 Paul's passionate and poetic language gives strong expression to his view of a Christian community. Few things brought Paul greater happiness than seeing a community living this kind of fellowship. What I translate as "fellow souls" is a beautiful word in Greek, *sumpseuchoi,* literally "with-souls."

2 Christian spirituality develops various conceptions of the goal of Christian life and practice. One classic form of Christian spirituality describes that goal as becoming an *alter Christus*, another Christ. Humility and concern for the interests of others, the ideas Paul focused on in the closing words of this passage, reflect central characteristics of Jeshu's life and ministry, characteristics that can take people, whether in Paul's time or ours, far along the path of becoming an *alter Christus*.

☐ True Fellowship

If you find encouragement in the Messiah, if you find loving comfort, if you find spiritual fellowship, if you find altruistic compassion, then fill up my cup of joy by being of one mind, sharing one love, living as fellow souls with a common understanding.[1] Don't act out of selfish rivalry or from boastfulness. Be truly humble in seeing others as better than yourselves. I don't want to see each of you looking out only for your own interests but rather concerning yourself about the interests of others.[2]

—PHILIPPIANS 2:1–4

1 This is a beautiful and insightful summary of spiritual practice. It involves right thought ("fill your minds") as well as right action ("do those things"). An ancient Buddhist text reminds us that our lives follow our thoughts the way a cart follows the oxen pulling it. Our world is an interpreted world, and we have choices about those interpretations. Paul recognizes that we can direct our attention to healthy and healing thoughts, just as we can choose to focus on what is pathological, upsetting, and hurtful.

If our minds are filled with the good things Paul talked about, then we stand a better chance of actually doing them, embracing a way of living in the world that the members of his communities not only heard from him but also saw through his example.

And the fruit of all of this is experiencing the God of peace and the peace of God. Not the superficial peace that comes from having things go our way, but the deeper peace that comes from having things go God's way.

☐ Right Thought and Right Action

I encourage you, my good friends, to fill your minds with whatever is true, God-centered, holy, beautiful, and worthwhile. Think about all those things that are virtuous and praiseworthy. And then do those things that you've learned and received from me, the things you've heard and seen in me. In this way the God of peace will be with you.[1]

—PHILIPPIANS 4:8–9

1 Paul didn't simply mention being "joyful in the Lord" in passing, as part of a long list of virtues. He singled it out, telling the Philippians that he couldn't possibly give enough emphasis to this practice. Distinct from merely having fun or being in a good mood, such joy, like deep peace of the soul, springs from a profound trust in God. One can know joy and peace at all times only by having a great faith that this moment, this here and now, is a divine invitation to grow, to learn, and to love.

2 Paul claimed that it was by their kindness, more than by their creeds or liturgies, that his fellow Christians should be recognized. The cruelty so often perpetrated in the name of religion—crusades, hate crimes—demonstrates a lack of compassion that flaunts the very core of Christ's (and Paul's) teachings.

3 Paul meant this in a literal, historical sense. Today, there are still Christians who cobble together a variety of biblical passages to project a timetable for Jeshu's return. Many other contemporary Christians, however, reject such literalism, understanding this language existentially, as describing an essential component of all human experience: There are no guarantees about tomorrow. As the Rabbis of antiquity said in their great wisdom: repent one day before you die.

4 Paul encouraged praying in a spirit of gratitude, being thankful even in expressing one's needs. This gratitude before our prayers are answered exhibits a trust that God understands our true needs better than we do.

5 Adepts in all the sacred traditions describe a profound peace as a constant in their experience. When asked whether anything ever disturbs his peace of soul, the Dalai Lama responded in the negative. St. Teresa of Ávila, one of the giants in the Christian mystical tradition, wrote that she reached a point where she experienced a deep peace that none of the circumstances of her life could shake.

☐ Joy, Peace, and Compassion

Always be joyful in the Lord. I can't emphasize this enough: be joyful.[1]
People outside the community should be able to recognize you by your
kindness.[2] The Lord is near.[3] Don't worry about things. Make all your
prayers and requests in a spirit of gratitude, letting God know what
you need.[4] And God's peace, which is beyond human comprehension,
will keep your hearts and minds safe in Ieshu the Messiah.[5]

—PHILIPPIANS 4:4–7

1 Paul reminded the members of the community in Rome that the sign by which their love for one another could be recognized was sincere respect. Such respect was more than propriety for Paul; it was based on the realization that, together with the Risen Christ, they constituted one body.

2 Paul drew a distinction here and in other passages in his letters between the loving behavior shown to fellow Christians ("being attentive to the needs of all the members of the community") and the love ("hospitality") that Christians extended to outsiders. It was only within the body constituted by community members and the Risen Christ that the fullness of love could be experienced.

3 Paul's words in this passage echoed some of Jeshu's most challenging teachings, especially not paying back evil with evil (Matt. 5:38) and loving one's enemies (Matt. 5:44).

4 Paul understood that the result of implementing these teachings in one's life was the experience of a profound peace. Paul further realized that it was only from the vantage point of that personally experienced peace that the members of his community could further strive "to live in peace with everyone."

☐ Learning to Live in Peace

Have real love for one another. Reject what is evil and hold on to what is good. Your love will be recognized by the sincere respect you show to one another.[1] Serve the Lord by constant dedication, spiritual enthusiasm, joyful hope, patient suffering, and persevering prayer. Be attentive to the needs of all the members of the community and reach out to strangers with your hospitality.[2] Say good things about those who persecute you. Don't call down curses on them but pray that God bless them.[3] Share the joy of those who are happy and the grief of those who mourn. Live with one another in peace. Don't be snobs; show the spirit of fellowship to those who aren't important in the world's eyes. Don't grow a big head. Don't pay back evil with evil; stay on the higher ground. To the extent that you can, live in peace with everyone.[4]

—ROMANS 12:9–18

1 Paul had a magnificent vision of the Christian community as a circle of faith in which the Spirit's gifts could be shared. Each person had one or more gifts, and each gift was for the building up of the community. The richness of community life rested on the mutuality of giving and receiving these gifts.

2 There's a difference between wisdom and knowledge. Knowledge may be a correct piece of information, but wisdom is the vision that coordinates those pieces into a whole picture. We find ourselves in an "information age" where wisdom is rare. We can turn to the Internet for knowledge, but not for wisdom.

3 The gifts are different, but the Spirit is the same. This is the source of unity in the community: the diverse members with their variety of gifts working in the one Spirit for the building up of one community in love. This can only happen, however, when the false self is transcended and the God-centered self emerges. Thus, when the members of any group (whether businesses, schools, or churches) are not personally evolved, the formation of a true community is impossible. What results is merely a conglomeration of false selves.

☐ Many Gifts but One Spirit

Now there are many kinds of gifts but the same Spirit, many kinds of ministries but the same Lord, many kinds of activities but the same God who acts in all of them and in all of you.[1] The Spirit is manifested to each person for the harmony of the whole community. The Spirit gives a word of wisdom to one member, and the same Spirit gives a word of knowledge to another.[2] The Spirit gives different gifts to different people: faith, the working of miracles, prophecy, the discernment of spirits, speaking in tongues, interpreting what is spoken in tongues. It's one and the same Spirit active in all these ways, giving each individual what the Spirit chooses to give.[3]

—1 CORINTHIANS 12:4–11

1 Paul's basic message was that Christians should live in peace with civil authorities, recognizing that all authority comes from God. Paul didn't want to bring suspicion to either his message or his communities. And since, from Paul's apocalyptic perspective, history was rapidly coming to an end, living in peace with the civil authorities seemed to be the best advice for the interim.

But Paul's context-bound statement that resistance to legal authority meant opposing God soon became inspired scripture. The danger inherent in Paul's position has haunted Christian history, for when there is no challenge to the uses of power, abuses are not far behind.

2 This sentiment that the authorities never create problems for good people betrays a political naiveté in Paul, unless we can presume that he was merely trying to render the potentially hostile empire benevolent. History is replete with civil authorities constituting a problem for good behavior—from harassing and arresting citizens for hiding escaped slaves to increasing burdensome taxes in order to wage unjust wars.

3 This may not be an accurate portrayal of the world as it existed then or now, but it might reflect Paul's hopes and prayers for a world in which the moral aims of religious and civil life would be consonant.

☐ Life in Caesar's Empire

Obey the authorities, since whatever authorities exist have been set up by God, since God is the source of all authority. To resist authority is to oppose what God has set up and to incur God's judgment.[1] The authorities don't constitute a problem for good conduct but for illegal behavior.[2] If you want to live with the approval of the authorities, then behave yourselves and you will gain that approval, since the authorities serve God in working on your behalf. But if you break the law, then you have good reason to fear the authorities, since they wield the power of punishment. They serve God by turning their anger against wrongdoers. Your obedience to these authorities should not be simply because you fear their anger but because of your own consciences. It's the same with paying taxes. The authorities are God's servants in being diligent about collecting taxes. Pay all of them their due—taxes to whom taxes are due, revenue to whom revenue is due, respect to whom respect is due, honor to whom honor is due.[3]

—ROMANS 13:1–7

1 Perhaps, when Paul said that they have been taught this by God, he was thinking of Leviticus 19:18, "Love your neighbor as yourself." After all, both Paul and Jeshu claimed that loving one's neighbor was synonymous with fulfilling the Torah.

2 Was this love for everyone, or was it restricted to fellow Christians? Probably the latter. Love, the Spirit's greatest gift, was to characterize members of these new communities of faith in their interactions with one another. What Paul urged these fledgling Christians to extend to outsiders was a reserved civility. Such behavior can certainly be construed as a form of love, but not love in its fullness.

Why did Paul recommend this quasi-isolation ("remaining independent")? Perhaps because he knew that his communities operated from principles radically different from the mores of civil society. God's reign invited people to a life that in every major respect contradicted the demands of Caesar's.

Christians challenged Caesar's reign by quietly but courageously embracing a radically different kind of life. The very existence of Christians as members of an alternative community was both an invitation and a challenge to those who found Caesar's reign attractive. On a practical level, Paul wanted Christians to live as independently as possible from the empire and its structures.

The two reigns still compete in our contemporary world. And Christians—from Quakers to Episcopalians—are challenged to find the form of community most facilitative of God's reign but most resistant to Caesar's.

☐ Living with Outsiders

You really shouldn't need anyone to write to you about loving one another, for this is something you have been taught by God.[1] Furthermore, I know that you do have love for all the members of the communities in Macedonia. All I can ask you, my dear friends, is to continue in this love, trying to live unobtrusively, minding your own business, working with your hands, as we have asked you to do in the past, conducting yourself civilly toward those outside our communities, while remaining independent of them.[2]

—1 THESSALONIANS 4:9–12

1 The Greek word here translated as "lacking motivation" is the most common word for being lazy or idle. But it's been said that being lazy means not being committed to someone else's agenda. So perhaps it is fairer to understand these community members simply as less motivated.

2 The injunction not to repay one bad action with another clearly echoes the teaching of Jeshu about loving one's enemies (Matt. 5:44). The whole point, of course, is not to have enemies, not to divide the world up with those categories.

People who regularly choose "bad actions" manifest a poorly informed conscience, which in turn presumes an insufficiently evolved consciousness. This is why Jeshu said to the Roman soldiers who drove nails into his wrists and ankles: "Heavenly Parent, forgive them, because they don't really know what they are doing" (Luke 23:34). All perpetrators of evil at some level really don't know what they are doing. Conscience never gets ahead of consciousness.

3 These three elements—the Spirit, prophecy, and discernment— belong together. God's Spirit is the source of all truth. The true prophet speaks God's truth to injustice. And discernment is what helps us distinguish the true prophet from the false.

☐ A Discerning Community

My dear brothers and sisters, I urge you to keep after the members of the community who lack motivation,[1] to cheer up those who are hesitant to act, to help the weak, and to be patient with everybody. Don't ever repay one bad action with another one. Always try to be altruistic, both toward members of the community and toward outsiders as well.[2] Always be joyful; always pray; always give thanks. This is God's will for you in Jeshu the Messiah. Don't extinguish the Spirit. Don't reject the prophets in your community. Be discerning in all matters. Stay with what is good and avoid all that is evil.[3]

—1 Thessalonians 5:14–22

1 This beautifully developed metaphor of a letter of recommendation eloquently speaks to Paul's closeness to the members of this community. They are no strangers to each other, needing the formalities of letters of recommendation and third-party testimonies. Jeshu the Messiah, Paul, and these Corinthians form one organic entity. God, God's Messiah, and God's Spirit constitute the very lifeblood of Paul and his communities.

Paul's language alludes to the great prophecy of Jeremiah 31:31–34, when God's law will be written on people's hearts, not as at Sinai, on tablets of stone. Humankind will one day evolve to a level of union consciousness in which the experience of the divine reality will be universal. Paul sees in his community an anticipation of this evolution.

☐ Paul's Love for His Communities

Does it sound like I'm bragging again? I don't think I need a letter of recommendation either to you or from you, as some strangers might. You are a letter of recommendation written on my heart, a letter that anyone can see and read. And your lives make it clear that you are indeed a letter of the Messiah, prepared by me, written not with ink but with the living God's Spirit, written not on stone tablets but on human hearts.[1]

—2 CORINTHIANS 3:1–3

1 One of the enduring strengths of Paul's theology is his sense of the organic unity of the Christian community with its Lord. The local community is the body whose head is the Messiah. This meant for Paul that every member of the community shared both in the experience of the head and in the experience of every other member. This is much like what happens when one part of us feels ill and that sense of dis-ease is immediately imparted to all parts of our body.

Jeshu the Messiah, the head of the community, experienced both the "fullness of suffering" and the "fullness of consolation." Thus, every member of the community was called to participate in that same fullness, knowing both the agony of the Messiah's death and the joy of his resurrection.

Paul saw this same pattern in his own life, and he told the Corinthians that they could learn this truth from him, just as he learned it from Jeshu the Messiah. For it was the same lifeblood of human experience, both in suffering and in consolation, that flowed in Jeshu, in Paul, and in each member of the community in Corinth.

☐ Individual and Community

Blessed be the God and Parent of our Lord Jeshu the Messiah, the Source of compassion and the God of all consolation. This is the God who consoles us in our troubles so that we may console others in trouble with the same consolation with which God consoles us. For just as we know the fullness of suffering in the Messiah, so too do we know in the Messiah the fullness of consolation. If we are suffering, it is for your consolation and healing. If we are being consoled, this too is for your consolation, the consolation you experience when you patiently bear up with the same sufferings we are experiencing. Our hope for you doesn't change. We know that you share both in our sufferings and in our consolation.[1]

—2 CORINTHIANS 1:3–7

1 Some of the Corinthian Christians had misunderstood Paul, thinking that he meant that they should avoid contact with all immoral people. But Paul was asking them to avoid contact with fellow Christians who behaved immorally.

We can see the premises of Caesar's reign in the vices Paul listed. Being greedy reflected seeing possessions as of utmost importance; worshipping idols included the cult of the emperor as God's Son.

2 The exclusion Paul recommended may well have constituted a form of what will later be understood as excommunication. It certainly brought a form of social pressure on the miscreants.

3 This business of judging is tricky. Jeshu taught his disciples not to judge (Matt. 7:1). Presumably this meant not to judge another person's inward status in the sight of God. In other words, we can use the word *sinner* only in the first person. This does not, however, preclude external kinds of judgment, such as a teacher giving a failing grade to a student.

Paul clearly believed the community members should judge those who behaved immorally. What is unclear, however, is whether Paul wanted this judgment to stop at external behavior or somehow reach to the very depths of an individual and thus constitute a judgment on how that person stood before God.

4 Paul could have been thinking of various texts here, such as "So you shall purge the evil from your midst" (Deut. 13:5). The challenge to the contemporary reader of Paul (and of Deuteronomy) stems from realizing our essential inability to identify "the wicked." We refrain from calling our children "bad boys and girls." Shouldn't this same restraint exist with older "children" (adults who are stuck at certain developmental stages)? We can certainly judge their behavior to be wrong, but are we ever in a position to judge their deepest interior state?

☐ Judging Community Members

I wrote to you earlier about not associating with sexually immoral people. I was not, however, referring to people outside our community. There is no way you can be in society and not associate with immoral people, with greedy people, with thieves, and with idol worshippers.[1] The point I want to make is not to associate with fellow Christians who are sexually immoral or greedy, who worship idols, put down others, get drunk, or rob other people. Don't even go out to dinner with members of the community who act like this.[2] I have nothing to do with judging those who are not members of our community. But don't you and I both have the obligation to judge those who are members of our community?[3] God will judge those who are outside our community. We read in scripture that we should drive out the wicked people from our community.[4]

—1 Corinthians 5:9–13

1 Just as a stone cannot absorb water, a life consciously dedicated to evil cannot be open to God's reign. That is the theme of this passage—people who deliberately choose evil are necessarily closed to the consciousness and conscience characterizing God's reign.

2 These catalogs of sin are sometimes difficult to translate. Since certain committed relationships between unmarried people may be moral, I use "sleep around" to stress the promiscuity of some sexual relations outside marriage.

3 The two Greek terms, *malakoi* ("men who live for pleasure" in my translation) and *arsenokoitai* (men who "prostitute themselves" in my translation), are virtually impossible to translate today with any degree of accuracy. The first term can refer to wine and music, as well as people, and indicated something soft. "Soft men" would probably be men given to hedonism. The second term referred to men having sex with other men, but the nature of the relationship was not specified. It most likely meant male prostitution.

It is important to remember that there was no general word for same-sex relations in the Greek vocabulary of Paul's time; a word inclusive of all same-sex relations does not occur in any language until the nineteenth century. So the shortest and, strictly speaking, the most accurate answer to the question "What does the Bible say about homosexuality?" is "Nothing." The current English-language Bibles translating these words as "homosexuals" are thus both incorrect and misleading.

If Paul intended to refer to all same-sex relations in using these terms, then he was making an unwarranted generalization. The emphasis of this passage is clearly on deliberate, destructive behavior, not on one's personal sexual preferences. We know of no instance where Jeshu or Paul dealt with a loving and committed same-sex couple and therefore have no solid basis for conjecturing about their possible views of such a relationship.

☐ Living Open to God's Reign

People consciously doing evil in the world cannot receive God's reign.[1] Don't let yourself be tricked in this regard. Those who sleep around with people to whom they are not married or with people who are married to someone else,[2] those who worship idols, men who live for pleasure or prostitute themselves,[3] thieves, the greedy, drunkards, those who put down other people, those who keep wanting more of everything — none of these will receive God's reign. Some of you once fit into one or other of these categories. But you have been baptized, made holy and God-centered in the name of the Lord Jeshu the Messiah and in the Spirit of our God.

—1 CORINTHIANS 6:9–11

1 Paul further developed in this passage his analogy of the body and its parts. Ambassadors were people like Paul who opened up mission fields, establishing and leading new communities. Prophets were not people who predicted the future so much as members of the community who spoke God's Word in the context of current situations, calling community members to act justly. Teachers explained the texts and traditions they had received. Miracle workers manifested God's power in everyday life. Healers brought wholeness to bodies and souls. Those who spoke in tongues were thereby prayerfully immersed in God's Spirit. The interpreters of tongues could discern a divine message in the foreign-sounding words. By thus developing the analogy, Paul helped us understand that these gifts of the Spirit are indeed as diverse and yet complementary as the different parts of our body.

☐ Members of One Body

Together you constitute the Messiah's body and individually you are its parts. God has appointed in the community first ambassadors, then prophets, teachers, miracle workers, healers, helpers, leaders, speakers in tongues. Not everyone is an ambassador. Not everyone is a prophet. Not everyone is a teacher. Not everyone works miracles. Not everyone is a healer. Not everyone speaks in tongues. Not everyone interprets tongues. But always try to attain the most important gifts, and I will tell you about the most important gift of all.[1]

—1 CORINTHIANS 12:27–31

1 Like a play having no small roles, the body has no part not playing an important role for the functioning of the whole. The relational character of this image also provides an important corrective to much of our contemporary life, where, plugged into our electronic devices, we often find ourselves isolated from the kind of personal relations that make us truly human. People today often find themselves rootless, without real community.

2 Christians joined this body through baptism and the drinking of the one Spirit, the latter being a possible reference to the communion cup. Why did Paul ascribe such mystical significance to Christian rituals such as baptism and yet continue to see Jewish (and certainly pagan) rituals as purely external and ineffectual? Was this hypocritical on his part or simply an example of a bias that Paul was unable to see? Given his lack of dialogical skills, I would surmise the latter.

In Galatians 3:28, Paul told us that in Christ there was no distinction between Jews and Greeks, slaves and free, males and females. But here, in speaking about becoming one body, Paul left out the third set of contraries. Since this image is anatomical, the omission of women seems ominously significant.

Paul was probably far more inclusive of women in ministry than most of his contemporaries. We know of at least one case (Rom. 16:7) where Paul referred to a certain woman named Junia (or Julia) as being "prominent among the ambassadors." In 1 Corinthians 12:28, Paul listed ambassadors as first among the gifts. So it may not surprise us that in many extant manuscripts, the female name has been replaced with a male name. This was probably just one example of other omissions or additions that crept into Paul's letters through copyists who were scandalized by his inclusion of women in ministerial roles. In fact, much of Paul's alleged misogyny may be attributable to some of his less honest editors rather than to Paul himself.

3 Paul was able to explain much of his ecclesiology (theology of church) by developing the image of the body and its various parts. There are three major lessons here: the diversity of gifts, the value of each gift, and their complementary character.

☐ Living as Part of the One Body

The Messiah is much like the human body, which is one but has many parts.[1] Our baptism in the one Spirit made us one body—Jews or Greeks, slaves or free—and we all drank the one Spirit.[2] The body has many parts. If the foot were to claim that, because it is not a hand, it does not belong to the body, that wouldn't change the fact that it is a part of the body. If the ear were to claim that it is not a part of the body because it is not an eye, that wouldn't change the fact that it is a part of the body. If the whole body were an eye, how would we hear? If the whole body were an ear, how would we be able to smell anything? But the way things are, God has arranged the parts of the body, each to be what God chose it to be.[3]

—1 CORINTHIANS 12:12–18

1 Paul laid down a guideline very helpful to conscience formation. One may be free to do or not to do something but may limit that freedom out of sensitivity to someone else who is less evolved spiritually.

2 Paul felt free to eat whatever was put before him. Nevertheless, if a dinner guest was concerned that the meat had been offered in sacrifice to an idol, then Paul passed up the meat course that night. This provides an enduring insight into conduct sensitive to others. My Jesuit high school religion teacher told us, back in the days when Catholics abstained from meat on Fridays, that if we were guests in a non-Catholic home on a Friday and a meat entrée was served, it was better to eat the meat than embarrass the host by calling attention to our abstinence.

3 Paul wanted to make it clear that he was not limiting his own freedom of conscience in making a decision to pass up the meat course when someone else might take offence. He still maintained his own freedom to eat whatever he wanted as long as he blessed God and acted for God's glory in all that he ate or drank, indeed in all that he did. What he demonstrated above all was what true freedom of conscience really meant.

☐ True Freedom of Conscience

Something may be lawful but not beneficial to others, legal but not helpful to others. Be aware of what is being done in the interest of others, not just what is done out of self-interest.[1] You're free to eat anything sold in the meat markets without any qualms of conscience, for "the earth is the Lord's and all that is in it." If you're invited to dinner by an unbeliever and decide to accept the invitation, eat whatever is served without any qualms of conscience. But if someone tells you that the meat has been offered in sacrifice, then don't eat it. This is not because of your conscience but because of the conscience of the person who told you this.[2] There's no reason my own freedom of conscience should be compromised because of someone else's conscience. If I bless the meat that's put before me, no one should condemn me because of what I bless. So in whatever you eat or drink or in whatever else you do, always act for God's glory.[3]

—1 CORINTHIANS 10:23–31

1 This text is often quoted as a Christian version of karma. Karma is the law of cause and effect, and similarly Paul stated quite clearly that whatever we plant in our garden is what we will harvest.

2 Although not entirely consistent in his use of language (few people are), Paul usually used the word *Flesh* not as a synonym for the body but as a word to name a dysfunctional relationship to some aspect of the human world because of a limited consciousness. This could mean a wrong understanding of sex, money, food and drink, human relationships—in short, anything pertaining to our life in the world.

Paul told us through his gardening analogy that if we thought about things in the wrong way, then we would inevitably act in the wrong way, and the results of our actions would be wrong as well.

Instead of realizing how our wrong orientation leads to wrong results, we can all too easily fall into the victim role, not recognizing the simple law of cause and effect. There's a story of a construction worker who unpacked his lunch and said to his fellow workers, "A cheese sandwich again." He made this same complaint several days in a row. Finally, one of his colleagues asked him why he didn't ask his wife to make him a different kind of sandwich. The man responded, "I don't have a wife; I make my own sandwiches."

3 Paul's perseverance in the face of obstacles is admirable. He knew full well that we can easily grow "tired of doing what is right" and "give up." People are eager to sign up for worthwhile projects, but after a few months, the list of volunteers is invariably shorter. Paul spent a long life facing shipwreck, stonings, hatred, and a great deal of jail time, but he ran his course with courage and steadfastness. In this respect, he is a great model for anyone walking a spiritual path.

☐ Christian Karma

Don't fool yourself. You can't make a fool out of God. Whatever grows in your garden is going to be what you planted there.[1] If you plant Flesh, then Flesh corruption is what will grow. [2] But if you plant Spirit, then Spirit life is what will grow. So don't grow tired of doing what is right because we will harvest what we've planted, as long as we don't give up.[3]

—GALATIANS 6:7–9

1 To love God is to be God-centered. Our false self must die into the larger identity of a God-centered self. From the more limited perspective of the false self, things are going wrong all the time. But for those who find their identity in God and want life to go God's way, every moment gives them an opportunity to learn or do something to help God's will to be done "on earth as it is in heaven" (Matt. 6:10b). And that goal enables us to see everything in our lives as working together for good.

2 Paul was very concerned about opposing the view that we put ourselves into a right relationship with God by our performance. Parents will testify that they didn't start loving their children after they were born and started to smile at them; they loved them from the time they knew there was life in the womb. So, too, God "knew us before we were born" and didn't begin to love us only when our good conduct merited his attention.

3 Paul wanted above all to stress the fact that everything was gift, that everything began with God's initiative, not ours. But in articulating this position, Paul's language about predestination and God's foreknowledge wandered dangerously close to the denial of our free will. It's important to keep in mind that all words, even Paul's, are inadequate to describe life's deepest mysteries.

Far too many Christian theologians (including such giants as Augustine, Luther, and Calvin) followed the words rather than the mystery to which the words pointed. And that has led to the fear-filled world far too many Christians inhabit today. The way forward from that fear is best expressed in the last verse of this passage. It is best understood, however, as a statement, not a question. God is for everyone. And since nothing is stronger than God, we will all make it home.

☐ Free and Predestined

If you love God, everything in your life will work together for good.[1]
This is true for all those who love God, all those called according to
the divine plan. For God knew us before we were born, and he
predestined us to be like his Son so that Jeshu might be the firstborn of
many siblings. God has called all those God has predestined; and God
has made God-centered all those God called; and God has called to
glory all those God made God-centered.[2] What should our reaction be
to all of this? If God is for us, who can be against us?[3]

—ROMANS 8:28–31

1 In what sense did God give up his Son for us? The words pull us into a morass of problems. Many of these have become beliefs for numerous Christians. First, Adam and Eve's sin got us into a lot of trouble: original sin. Second, God was angry and needed to be placated. Third, no ordinary human could do this, so God sent his Son. Fourth, atonement for sin demanded blood. Fifth, God's Son died a bloody death on the cross as an atonement sacrifice. Sixth, only those who believe all of the above can be saved.

Like many contemporary Christian theologians, I cannot accept any of these six beliefs. So what alternative belief system can I propose that in any way seems consonant with Paul? First, we all struggle to grow up spiritually. Second, God is totally with us in this struggle. Third, Jeshu's faithful life and death can be a tremendous source of help in growing spiritually. Fourth, our sins are always trumped by God's infinite love and forgiveness, and Jeshu taught us that lesson in many ways. Fifth, Jeshu died a bloody death on the cross because his message flew in the face of the vicious and cruel empire of Rome. Sixth, no matter what we believe, we will all eventually be saved because there's no other way for the story to end if it includes an all-loving God at its beginning.

2 I use legal terminology to translate some of these Greek words because Paul used a courtroom scene as an extended image in this passage. Who would dare step forward as the prosecuting attorney when Jeshu himself is our defense lawyer?

3 God loves the members of the Messiah's community, and the Messiah himself loves the members of his community. This covenanting love is what binds Christians together and what makes them ultimately invincible. Yet this is only one way of telling the story. Other ways are valid too, as long as all the stories understand that God wins in the end.

☐ Relationship to the Risen Messiah

Since God didn't hold back from giving up his own Son for us, do you think that God would hold back from giving us everything else?**1** Is there anyone out there wanting to bring charges against God's chosen ones? It is God after all who makes all relationships right. Who wants to be our prosecutor? The one defending us is the Messiah Jeshu who indeed died but was then raised from the dead to be at God's right hand.**2** Who or what can pull us away from the love the Messiah has for us? How about hardships, anguish, persecution, famine, nakedness, dangers, wars? We read in the Psalms: "For your sake we are being killed all day long; our enemies think of us as sheep to be slaughtered." In the face of all of these problems we come out victorious because of the one who loved us. I am convinced that neither death, life, angels, cosmic forces, present enemies, enemies to come, powers, spirits on high, spirits below, nor anything else in creation can separate us from the love God has for us in the Messiah Jeshu our Lord.**3**

—ROMANS 8:32–39

1 Some scholars have suggested that this part of the text may have been a hymn sung by Christians and used here by Paul. But whether Paul was repeating others' views or expressing his own, we can certainly presume that this is what he believed regarding the identity of Jeshu the Messiah. Its central thesis is Jeshu's self-emptying, or *kenosis* in Greek. This word has entered theological conversation, and we can speak today of a kenotic way of living as not clinging to rank or privilege, to power or prestige.

2 The cosmic geography of Paul and his peers was a tripartite one. Imagine it as a three-layer cake. There was heaven, the earth, and the underworld. Jeshu's career was a participation in all three worlds. He originated in the heavenly realm (with a divine form); came down to the earthly realm (taking on human form); descended into the underworld (after his death); returned to the earthly realm (in his resurrection); and finally returned to the heavenly realm (in his ascension).

Since we no longer live in this kind of cosmos, some Christians feel a need to rethink our language regarding the question of Jeshu's identity. Unfortunately, popular Christian belief often fails to do that, leaving us with strange scenarios of Jeshu going up to heaven on clouds, even though our universe has no "up," and clouds wouldn't get you very far in any case.

The words—whether from Paul or from an inherited hymn—suggest a divine being in the heavenly realm emptying himself of his divinity. This image is problematic for some Christians today. But however one chooses to unpack the symbolic language, Christians would agree that Jeshu lived his life as a vulnerable human being striving to serve God by serving others. And this, in the long run, is what is important for anyone who regards Jeshu as model and mentor in the quest for God-centeredness.

☐ The Identity of Jeshu the Messiah

You should think about things in the same way that Jeshu the Messiah did. He had at his disposal the form of God, but he didn't regard this equality with God as something to be clung to. He emptied himself, taking the form of a servant and becoming like any other human being.[1] Assuming human form, he humbled himself, obedient to God in life and in death, even death on a cross. And this is why God raised him up, giving him a name that excels all other names, so that when the name of Jeshu is heard, all should fall to their knees—those in heaven, those on earth, and those in the underworld.[2] And everyone should acknowledge that Jeshu the Messiah is Lord, to the glory of God our heavenly Parent.

—PHILIPPIANS 2:5–11

1 Paul was in jail where a slave, probably an escaped slave, helped him, perhaps after Paul initiated him into Christian fellowship. Paul asked Philemon, the slave's owner, to take this slave back as a fellow Christian or perhaps allow the slave to stay with Paul, continuing to help him as long as he remained in jail.

2 Paul was punning with the meaning of the slave's name. Onesimus means "useful." The church historian Eusebius tells us that there was an early bishop of Ephesus named Onesimus. This is probably the slave-turned-bishop referred to in this text, which would certainly explain why this is the only one of Paul's personal letters preserved. The bishop would surely not have allowed his own story to be lost.

3 No text in the Christian Testament condemns slavery. And yet, thoughtful Christians must have sensed some problems in a system where human beings were bought and sold like cattle. But even if they experienced some cognitive dissonance, neither Paul nor the members of his communities had the leverage for starting an abolitionist movement. Paul's solution was to play down the physical (i.e., political and economic) reality of slavery and speak to the spiritual dimension of the master/slave relationship. Philemon and other slave-holding Christians were called to treat their slaves as brothers and sisters.

4 Why could Paul not come straight out and ask Philemon (and other slave-holding Christians) to release their slaves, hiring them as free workers if that proved mutually agreeable? Perhaps because of his eschatological belief that the end of present history was at hand and it therefore made no sense to waste time changing sociological structures. Or perhaps because of Paul's philosophical inclination to ignore or downplay the physical dimension of life, while focusing on the spiritual side. In either case, Paul's failure to take the next logical step in implementing Jeshu's teachings contributed to the horror of slavery lasting for many centuries longer in Christian societies. This is one place where Paul's teaching, laudable in its time, cried for the amendment provided by subsequent history.

☐ More Than a Slave

I am pleading on behalf of my child, Onesimus, whose father I have become during my time here in jail.[1] He may have been useless to you at some point, but he's certainly useful now to both of us.[2] I'm sending him back to you, even though I feel like I'm sending part of my heart. Part of me wants to keep him here with me, where his service can substitute for your service during my jail time for proclaiming the good news. But I don't want to do anything without your consent because I want you to be acting freely and not under pressure. Maybe this is the reason for his being away from you for a while so that you can have him back permanently, not as a slave anymore but more than a slave, a brother you love.[3] He is very much a brother to me and how much more so to you, both physically and spiritually.[4]

—PHILEMON 1:10–16

The Lord's Supper

1 Paul stated that when we "give thanks" with the cup of blessing and when we "break" the bread, we enjoyed fellowship in the blood and the body of the Messiah. Notice the dynamic quality of this language. Paul was not talking about bread and wine as static objects being somehow turned into body and blood. Paul used relational terms ("giving thanks with the cup" and "breaking the bread"). In other words, Paul's language did not focus on the sacramental elements (bread and wine) but on the sacramental actions (giving thanks, pouring wine, and breaking bread).

2 The tradition seems unassailable that Jeshu shared bread and wine with his disciples on the evening of his arrest. But what meaning did he give to this last supper? Paul suggested that the community members' participation in this ritual made them somehow one, just as the bread is one.

But what about the later theological language claiming that we eat the Messiah's body and drink his blood? An immediate problem arises in the context of Judaism, where one of the most basic principles of kashrut (the laws regarding what food can be eaten and the proper preparation of permitted food) is the avoidance of any consumption of blood. Any connection of blood and drinking is indescribably repugnant in a Jewish context.

Paul undoubtedly saw the death of Jeshu as a sacrifice. The two elements used in the ritual (bread and wine) suggest separation; and the separation of the bread and wine suggests the separation of body and blood in a sacrificial death. Thus, the participants in the meal had a fellowship with Jeshu's sacrifice by eating the bread and drinking the wine.

Pouring and breaking meaningfully suggest a sacrificial death: a life poured out for others, broken for others. So sharing the meal means recognizing the sacrificial character of all true love. And sharing in the meal means sharing in the community's commitment to love faithfully, even unto death. And it's in that life of faithful love that the community is indeed one with its Lord.

☐ Fellowship with the Messiah

When we give thanks with the cup of blessing, isn't this fellowship in the blood of the Messiah? And when we break the bread, isn't this fellowship in the body of the Messiah?[1] Because the bread is one and because we eat the one bread, we are one body, however many of us there are.[2]

—1 CORINTHIANS 10·16–17

1 Jewish days begin at sunset, so Sunday begins at sunset on Saturday, when the Sabbath ends. This transition from the Sabbath to the weekday world is marked by the Jewish ritual called Havdalah (from the root word meaning "to separate"). So it was when the Sabbath was over with Saturday's sunset that the Christian communities gathered to celebrate the Lord's Supper. From the modern Christian perspective, that would be Saturday evening, but from the perspective of the Jewish calendar, it would already be Sunday.

2 The original celebration of the Lord's Supper was the ancestor of the potluck dinner. Members of the community brought food and drink. The wealthier members, of course, had the opportunity to bring better provisions, while the poor were only able to bring very little or nothing at all.

This common meal was meant to ensure that even the poorest members of the community had one good meal a week. But if the rich ate the good food they brought before the poor even arrived, it left the poor with very little. Paul was clearly upset with this total perversion of the whole idea of a communal meal.

These abuses of the meal aspect of the Lord's Supper soon led Christian communities to separate the Communion from partaking in a full meal. The increased size of Christian communities led to this change in practice as well. Today, the eating and drinking is quite modest, usually nothing more than a bite-size piece of bread and a tiny glass of wine or grape juice.

But even though one kind of abuse has been eliminated, this does not mean that privilege no longer has an influence. One priest told me that a woman in his parish would put a check for one thousand dollars in the collection if she agreed with the sermon, but nothing if she didn't. Wealth and prestige still can stain the equality that Paul desired among the members of his churches.

☐ Privilege and the Lord's Supper

I wonder whether or not when you come together on Sundays, it's really to eat the Lord's Supper.[1] For when it's time to eat, some of you proceed to eat what you brought with you while others go hungry and yet still others are getting drunk. What's the matter with you? Don't you have homes where you can eat and drink? Don't you realize that you're mocking the community of God and humiliating the poor? What can I say about this? Do you expect to be congratulated? I'm not about to congratulate you about this.[2]

—1 CORINTHIANS 11:20–22

1 Paul frequently distinguished material that came from the Lord (either by direct revelation to him or through a tradition directly linked to Jeshu) and material that reflected his own thoughts and ideas. Here, he was quite explicit in stating that this tradition was from the Lord. Since it was, however, a tradition (something "passed on"), we are led to conclude that it did not come to Paul through direct revelation but was mediated by others.

2 Paul is the earliest source for what happened at that last meal that Jeshu shared with his disciples, but his narrative is fraught with problems. Could Jeshu really have identified bread with his body and invited his disciples to eat it? Or identified wine with his blood and invited his disciples to drink it? This seems impossible in terms of Jewish sensitivity to consuming even the blood of an animal, let alone that of human beings.

Could this whole idea of drinking blood have come from Paul's experience with mystery cults in which the blood of animals was drunk? We will perhaps never know. What we do know is that there were early Christian communities who interpreted this meal quite differently. The *Didache*, a church manual from the end of the first century, describes a Eucharist but with no reference to sacrifice or death. Instead, the emphasis is on community: the grapes make one wine, the grains of wheat make one bread. Other traditions ignored it completely. In the 114 sayings attributed to Jesus in the Gospel of Thomas, there is no reference to a final supper. But Paul's interpretation, which filters into Mark, Matthew, and Luke, clearly reflected the sacrificial metaphor so central to his thinking.

Many contemporary theologians, while appreciating the metaphors that moved Paul, are exploring new ways to understand this last meal of Jeshu with his disciples. Perhaps it is above all else a fellowship in a way of living and loving in the world that calls the participants to a faithfulness to death in following the path of selfless service to others. In that sense, every truly Christian life is one poured out in service and broken in the acceptance of the suffering involved in any life dedicated to love.

☐ The Revealed Story

The Lord himself is the source of what I'm passing on to you,[1] namely, that the Lord Jeshu, on the night he was handed over, took bread, blessed it, broke it, and said, "This is my body that is for you. Do this in my memory." And in the same way, after the supper, he took the cup and said, "This cup is the new covenant in my blood. As often as you drink it, do this in my memory." As often as you eat this bread and drink from this cup, you announce the Lord's death until his coming.[2]

—1 CORINTHIANS 11:23–26

Jews and
Christians

1 If we understand Torah-works as actions motivated by nothing more than not breaking a law, then it's clear that this kind of activity cannot lead to God-centeredness. It's an attempt to back out of hell more than a commitment to move forward on a path of love. Faith-works, on the other hand, are actions motivated by trust in the divine reality—whether that is conceptualized as God, the Tao in Chinese thought, or Wakan Tanka among some Native Americans. Thus, faith-works can and do lead to God-centeredness.

Having nothing more than the rules of any sacred tradition, we learn no more than the various ways in which rules can be broken. Knowing the law doesn't give us any real motivation for keeping the law, other than not wanting to get caught. Reading in the Bible that we should not be dishonest in our business practices might lead us to take steps not to be sent to prison like so many CEOs. But this kind of self-protective posturing falls short of virtue. On the other hand, someone who recognizes one divine reality as the source of every person on the planet and who sincerely strives to live in such a way as to treat others like brothers and sisters is clearly on a path to a God-centered life.

Although understanding the text this way makes sense to many of us today, it may not reflect all that Paul was implying. Paul's exclusivism did not allow for many forms of faith-works, because it did not allow for many forms of faith. For Paul, the Torah cannot be lived faithfully without faith in Jeshu the Messiah; without this messianic interpretation, the Torah remains at the level of Sin and Flesh.

Thus, those Jews who try to relate to God through the nonmessianic Torah must inevitably fail and fall short. Paul rightly put his finger on the difference between law-works and faith-works operative in any religious context, but he seemed unable to free that insight from the exclusivist lens through which he saw it. This is an instance where Paul's insight must be allowed to grow through the next two thousand years in which humankind has learned a lot more about the benefits of pluralism.

☐ Torah-works vs. Faith-works

No one will be God-centered by Torah-works, for all the Torah can do is teach us what is wrong.[1]

—ROMANS 3:20

1 For Paul, all human beings sin or miss the mark. Gentile sinners, not knowing the Torah, are not judged by the Torah. Presumably, they are judged by the standards applying to all people, the basic principles of morality. Jews, on the other hand, because they know the teachings of the Torah, have a higher moral responsibility and a higher standard by which they are judged. But Paul wanted to make it clear that Jews had no advantage simply in having heard the Torah. Their trust in the Torah had to be manifested by their obedience to its injunctions. The question left hanging in the air is whether any Jews can do what the Torah enjoins or whether any Gentiles can do what is required by basic morality.

☐ The Torah or Christ

All who have sinned without the Torah will also perish without the Torah, and all who have sinned with the Torah will be judged by the Torah. For it is not hearing the Torah that makes one God-centered but doing it.[1]

—ROMANS 2:12–13

1 When people want to convert to Christianity, do they first need to become Jews? Such a question would never be asked today. This is why it's difficult for us to realize how vital a question this was in the early days of Christianity. To most of the Jewish Christians at that time, especially the members of the Jerusalem community under Jacob, the obvious answer was yes. But for Paul, and certainly for other Christians who were either Hellenistic Jews or Gentiles, the answer was no.

The whole argument hinges on the distinction between moral commandments and holiness codes. Paul argued in Romans 13:8 that the person who loved his or her neighbor had fulfilled the Torah. This made sense in terms of the moral commandments, but it left out the holiness codes. Paul's premise was that Gentile converts should be bound by the moral codes but not by the holiness codes. And it is that premise that has dictated Christian practice to our own day.

Paul's passionate nature is revealed in this passage. Few things seemed to cause him more personal hurt than when Gentile Christians were made to feel as though they were second-class members of the community. Imagine how snubbed these Gentile Christians must have felt when Rock, one of Jeshu's chief disciples, no longer sat with them at dinner.

Table fellowship has always been significant as a marker of sociological lines of distinction. One has only to think of the lunch-counter sit-ins during the civil rights movement. Even today, dinner guests in a wealthy home would be stunned if the hostess invited the cook or butler to pull up a chair to the table. This conflict was serious enough for Paul to decide to sever his connection with the Antioch community forever.

☐ Charge of Hypocrisy

When Rock came to Antioch, I confronted him directly on a matter where he was clearly in the wrong. Until certain members of Jacob's community in Jerusalem came to Antioch, Rock would share table fellowship with the Gentile Christians. But after the delegation from Jerusalem arrived, he pulled back and avoided table fellowship with the Gentile Christians out of fear of the Circumcision Party. The other Jewish Christians joined him in this hypocrisy, and even Barnabas was duped. But realizing that they were not acting in a way that was consistent with the truth of the good news we were announcing, I said to Rock in front of the whole community: "If you, as a Jew, are living like a Gentile and no longer as a Jew, what right do you have to require Gentile converts to live like Jews?"[1]

—GALATIANS 2:11–14

1 Many would see this passage as universalist and all-embracing. And, in one sense, it is. No difference between Jewish or Gentile Christians; no difference between slave or free Christians; no difference between male and female Christians. This is revolutionary, whether in Paul's time or in our own.

There is another perspective, however, in which this passage is narrow and exclusivist. Are we sons and daughters of God only through our faith in Jeshu? This is what Paul clearly stated here. But how, then, do we read the statement in Genesis 1:26 that all human beings are made in God's image and likeness? Aren't all human beings God's sons and daughters? Are we then God's children by our creation or only by membership in Paul's community of faith? Paul's exclusivism permeates this passage.

Replacement theology characterizes this text as well. Judaism cries out to be replaced by Christian faith. The time of the Torah was a time of external observance, of Torah-works, a time without faith. Everything was on hold until the Messiah's arrival. With the Messiah came faith, life, and the possibility of being God's children. The Torah, for Paul, was indeed a babysitter (a mere guardian or custodian). Only by faith in the Messiah can we begin our lives as real sons and daughters of God.

The challenge to today's faithful in all the sacred traditions is whether or not we will continue to define the community of believers solely in our own terms or whether we will do so more universally. To paraphrase one of the great mystic poets of Islam: How can we accept the sunlight coming in one window but deny that same sunlight when it comes through other windows?

☐ Community Beyond Boundaries

Before faith came, we were held as prisoners and guarded under the Torah until faith was revealed. So the Torah was like a babysitter taking care of us until the Messiah came and we could be God-centered through faith. But with the arrival of faith, we no longer need the babysitter. We are all sons and daughters of God through our faith in Jeshu the Messiah. By being immersed in the Messiah, you are clothed in the Messiah. It is no longer important whether you are a Jew or a Gentile, a slave or a free person, a male or a female. You are all one in Jeshu the Messiah.[1]

—GALATIANS 3:23–28

1 Paul's mysticism shines through his passage. When Paul was living most deeply, it was not his ego that drove his decisions and actions but the divine mystery revealed in the person of Jeshu. This mystic testimony is pointed and powerful.

But, as happens so often with Paul, the purity of his mystical voice seems diminished by his exclusivism. Why did Paul derive from his own mystical experience of God in Jeshu the Messiah the belief that others cannot find God-centeredness through the Torah, through the Qur'an, or through the teachings of the Buddha?

2 Perhaps his interpretation of the Messiah's death constituted the stumbling block to a more pluralistic understanding on Paul's part. If God-centeredness could come in any other way than through the Messiah, then "the Messiah died for no reason." In Paul's mind, what indeed was the "reason" for which the Messiah died? To atone for humankind's sins or Sin. This is why the Messiah "gave himself up for me." But in that case, no one else can atone for these sins, and therefore, there is no one else in whom there can be salvation.

And there's the rub. If Paul was wrong about human beings needing to be saved from Sin, then he was also wrong about his interpretation of Jeshu's death, and he was wrong too about the exclusivism of this path to salvation. Many contemporary Christian scholars do find Paul wrong on all three counts. While accepting Paul's mystical life in Jeshu the Messiah, they reject the exclusivist context in which he communicated that profound experience. In other words, they seek to define Paul by his lights, not by his limitations. And that, of course, is my purpose here as well.

□ No Salvation through the Torah

It's because of the Torah that the Torah is dead for me, so that I can be alive in God. I've been put on the cross with the Messiah. I'm no longer the one who is living; it is the Messiah who is living in me.[1] And my present life in the flesh is a life in faith, faith in God's Son who loved me and gave himself up for me. I'm not rejecting God's grace, for if God-centeredness came through the Torah, then the Messiah died for no reason.[2]

—GALATIANS 2:19–20

1 It is clear that Paul had a strong sense of the sinful state of the world. The fact that human beings sin, miss the mark, fail to reach their potential for wise and compassionate living, is recognized by virtually all the sacred traditions and indeed by anyone who reads a daily newspaper. If that were Paul's meaning, there would not be much disagreement.

But most of these same traditions that recognize sins also teach that human beings are essentially good, although needing to evolve in terms of their consciousness and conscience. Did Paul's position agree with this? Probably not. In addition to sins, Paul seemed to be convinced of a "power of sin" or a state or condition of sinfulness that, for clarity's sake, I call Sin.

With the words of this text, Paul may have sown the seed that, some four hundred years later, emerged as a plant in Augustine's garden. Augustine called it *peccatum originale*—original sin. Human nature is essentially sinful, evil, even depraved.

It is precisely this theology that is under siege today. An ontological depravity in human nature contradicts the enduring goodness of creation. And if Sin does indeed characterize human nature, and if Jesus is the sole cure for this predicament, then most of the millions of people who have gone before us are in hell and the same destiny awaits most people alive today. This contradicts the reality of a loving God.

If, on the other hand, the human condition is not inherently evil, but simply not developed, then Christian theology joins up with the majority of spiritual traditions. We are no more born spiritually mature than we are born physically mature. We need to grow up. Our growth, however, is from good to better, not from bad to good. Any exclusivity disappears from the Christian message, and the reign of God that Jesus proclaimed becomes good news for all human beings.

☐ Jews and Non-Jews Alike

Are we Jews better off than anyone else? Not in the least. I've already made the indictment that everyone, whether Jew or non-Jew, lives subject to the power of Sin. For we read in scripture, "No one is God-centered, not even one."[1]

—ROMANS 3:9–10

1 Paul took several scriptural passages out of context and used them to support his own, ultimately untenable, thesis. The most distressing part of Paul's argument was his creation of a dichotomy separating Torah observance and faith. This has led to the often-heard Christian comment: "Jews seek to be God-centered through works, but Christians are God-centered through faith."

2 Paul's admirable eagerness to proclaim that "the blessing of Abraham" has now come to the Gentiles through Jeshu the Messiah led him to deny any other access to this blessing, since only Paul and his fellow Christians accepted the divine initiative called grace. And yet, Jews speak of the "matan Torah"—the gift of the Torah. The Torah is Israel's grace. In that sense, grace—the divine initiative—comes first for Judaism just as it does for Paul.

Now there are those in every tradition who have a "gum ball" theology, namely, the idea that if you put in your quarter you get the divine prize. But wherever this viewpoint is found—whether among Jews, Christians, Buddhists, Hindus, or Muslims—it represents an immature understanding of religion. Paul led to the creation of this stereotype against Judaism, just as Luther and the other Reformers led to the creation of this same stereotype against Roman Catholicism.

Paul was right in asserting that law-works (the mere external conformity to a religious code) can't make people God-centered. Only faith-works lead to God-centeredness. But faith-works characterize deep Jewish life as much as they characterize deep Christian life. A truly Torah-observant life is based on a trust in the divine initiative every bit as much as a life authentically rooted in the teachings of Jeshu. And the same is true of a deep Muslim life, a deep Hindu life, or a deep Buddhist life.

☐ The Torah Is a Curse

Those living under the Torah are living under a curse, for it is written that "anyone not observing and obeying all that is in the Torah is cursed." It's clear that no one can be God-centered by the Torah, for it is also written that "the God-centered person lives by faith." But the Torah doesn't rest on faith.[1] For we read that "the one who does the works of the Torah will live by them." The Messiah delivered us from the curse of the Torah by becoming a curse for us, for it is written that "everyone who hangs on a tree is cursed." And this is all so that in Jeshu the Messiah the blessing of Abraham might come to the Gentiles and that we might receive the promised Spirit through faith.[2]

—GALATIANS 3:10–14

1 Paul's world is one in which few are saved, while most are moving toward destruction. This is a worldview that many Christians in Paul's day and in our own find unacceptable. If God does indeed love us more than we can love ourselves, then surely God can find a way to bring us all home.

Paul believed in the "wrath of God," a belief seen as inconsistent with the divine reality by many Christians today. Paul further believed in a punitive God who could send most human beings to inhabit an eternal hell. This, too, is rejected by many Christians today. There can be no permanent hell, no final alienation from the divine reality that is our deepest being. No one will be left behind. These ideas reflect Paul's limitations more than his central enlightenment.

2 Paul was certainly correct in asserting that much that the world (i.e., the socialized world or "Caesar's reign") considered wisdom was foolishness. And much that the world considered foolish was wise. The limitation of Paul's vision lay in thinking that only his personal path embodied God's wisdom and that all other paths, those of Jews and Gentiles alike, were foolish.

3 Paul's exclusivism is revealed again in this notion that only those who believed as he did could be saved. There is indeed a divine wisdom manifested in the crucified Christ, but it is manifested no less in the Torah, in the Qur'an, in the enlightened Buddha, and in countless other sacred traditions. Paul saw the validity only of his experience of the divine mystery, and this spiritual myopia continues to characterize the thinking of many Christians to this day.

4 In this passage, Paul used the words *Gentiles* and *Greeks* as synonyms. I use the word *Greeks* throughout to avoid possible confusion.

☐ The Cross Is the Only Wisdom

What we say about the cross is foolishness for those who are moving toward destruction, but for those of us who are being saved it is God's power.[1] We read in scripture: "I will destroy the wisdom of the wise; I will set aside the intelligence of the intelligent." Where is the wise person? Where is the Torah scholar? Where is the worldly pundit? Has not God shown the wisdom of this world to be foolishness?[2] For since it was God's wisdom that the world not know God through worldly wisdom, God decided to save believers through our message, which the world regards as foolishness.[3] Jews want miracles and Greeks want philosophy, but our message is a crucified Messiah, a scandal for the Jews and foolishness for the Greeks. But for all those called to the community of faith, whether Jews or Greeks, this crucified Messiah is God's power and wisdom.[4] For when God is foolish, God is still wiser than humans, and when God is weak, God is still stronger than humans.

—1 CORINTHIANS 1:18–25

1 Paul registered surprise that Gentiles could experience a relationship with God, while Jews could not. But this statement lacks some necessary nuances. *Some* Gentiles have found a relationship with God through their faith in Jeshu. No argument there. But how does Paul conclude that no Jews can experience a relationship with God through their lives of Torah observance?

This is based on Paul's separation of faith and works. If Jewish life were based on a faith in works alone, then indeed Jews could not be God-centered. But if Jews (at least some Jews) have faith in what God has revealed at Sinai and strive to live their lives accordingly, then why would those Jews not be God-centered? It must be because Paul came to believe that no other faith in God counted except for faith in Jeshu. And if that were indeed the case, then it follows that no Jews could be saved, nor anyone else who did not have faith in Jeshu. This presents us with Christian theology in its most exclusivist form.

A Christian pluralist, however, would argue that Christians do indeed find God-centeredness through their faith in Jeshu as the one who most reveals God and God's way to them. But they would see that same God-centeredness in their Jewish, Muslim, Buddhist, and Hindu brothers and sisters who have faith in or trust another path (the Torah, the Qur'an, and so forth) that connects them to the divine center.

The interplay of light and limit in Paul challenges the contemporary reader. He often began a line of thought with a genuine insight—for example, that Gentiles experienced God-centered lives through their faith in Jeshu the Messiah. But at that point his inherent inability to affirm any other view than his own led him to add the assertion that there was no other way of being God-centered.

It is a challenge to know how to read Paul. And yet, he may have given us a hint in his admission in 2 Corinthians 4:7 that the treasure of the good news he received was contained in the clay jar of his own humanness. The ultimate challenge to Paul's readers may be the task of extricating the treasure from the clay.

☐ A Surprise for Everyone

What can I say? Gentiles who weren't looking for God-centeredness have attained it, a God-centeredness based on faith, while Israel, who was looking for a God-centeredness based on the Torah, didn't attain it. Why not? Because they didn't seek it with faith but with the misunderstanding that it was based on works.[1]

—ROMANS 9:30–32A

1 The opening verse reflects a valid insight for any religious practice. Physical circumcision is a sign of a Jew's covenantal life with God. If a Jew lives with no covenantal life with God, then his physical circumcision has little meaning. It's like a married man wearing a wedding ring but consistently cheating on his wife.

2 The second verse is problematic. One of the most time-honored responses in debate is *datur tertium*: namely, there is a third option. When someone pressures us to choose between A and B, we can simply point to C as another option. If a male Jew obeys the Torah, then why would he not choose to be circumcised as a sign of his covenanted life with God? After all, being circumcised is part of obeying the Torah.

But Paul tried to drive a wedge between the physical and the spiritual when there is no need to separate the two. Why should a man be merely "considered" circumcised when he can choose actually to be circumcised? He can be physically circumcised *and* be spiritually circumcised as well: *datur tertium*.

3 This verse, like the first, makes some intuitive sense. Someone with an experienced relationship with God is further along than someone with the Torah scroll and physical circumcision but with no spiritual practice.

4 It is not something physical *alone* that makes someone Jewish, but something that is both physical and spiritual. The final verses bring us back to our *datur tertium* position. Why does Paul insist on seeing it as an either/or option? Paul tried very hard to make us choose between the physical and the spiritual.

Paul wanted us to identify Judaism without faith in Jeshu the Messiah as caught up in physical acts that did not access the spiritual realm. But we have to keep resisting Paul here, pointing out that this dichotomy is a false one. It makes as much sense for a Jew to be physically circumcised *and* lead a spiritual life as to wear a wedding band *and* be a faithful spouse.

☐ Circumcision

Circumcision has some value if you obey the Torah, but if you don't obey the Torah, then you might as well be uncircumcised.[1] And by the same token, shouldn't those who aren't circumcised but obey the Torah be considered circumcised?[2] So those who are physically uncircumcised but obey the Torah have every right to condemn you if you have both the Torah scroll and circumcision, but fail to obey the Torah.[3] For it is not something visible that makes someone Jewish nor is true circumcision something visible on a physical body. It is something hidden that makes someone Jewish, and real circumcision is something spiritual, not literal.[4]

—ROMAN 2:25–29

1 Moses was protecting the people from the glow of God's glory on his countenance. Paul's unusual interpretation has Moses trying to avoid having the people see that God's glory was diminishing. In other words, Paul was arguing that, already in Moses's time, the covenant of Sinai was "old" and inferior, pointing to a "new" covenant that would one day replace it.

2 This is classic replacement theology, a position that has tainted Jewish–Christian relations for centuries. It consists of the unwarranted assertion that Christianity has replaced Judaism and that a new covenant (New Testament) has superseded an old covenant (Old Testament).

Testamentum is the Latin word for "covenant." It is in this passage that the idea of an Old Testament was born. This is why it has become more common in interreligious dialogue today to avoid speaking of an Old and a New Testament, since that stems from replacement theology. Instead, we talk about the Hebrew Bible and the Christian Testament.

3 During my student days in Europe, I often saw the matching statues on the entrance to some of the medieval cathedrals. On one side was "Ecclesia," the church, a woman with a crown and a scepter. On the opposite side was "Synagoga," the synagogue, a woman blindfolded holding the broken tablets of the old covenant. These statues are a commentary in stone on this tragic verse robbing Judaism of its ongoing reality as a religion mediating a true relationship between the Jewish people and God.

Numerous churches today have repudiated this teaching, stating that God continues to be in relationship with Jews through the covenant of Sinai and that, therefore, Jews should not be missionized by Christians. This teaching is called "dual covenant" theology. We find in this theology an important amendment to Paul's thought, one desperately needed after two thousand years in which its absence led to such great suffering for the Jewish people.

☐ The Birth of the Old Testament

Our hope enables us to act with great boldness, unlike Moses, who
veiled his face to keep the Israelites from looking at the fading glory
that was being replaced.[1] But they were stubborn in their disbelief. Even
today when they hear the reading of the "Old Testament"[2] in their
synagogues, that same veil is still in place. For it is only in the Messiah
that the veil can be removed. So even today when the Torah is read, that
veil covers their minds, and it is only by turning to the Lord that the veil
can be removed.[3]

—2 CORINTHIANS 3:12–16

Teachings on
Sexuality

1 The Corinthians were undoubtedly Paul's most controversial community, torn by wildly divergent factions. Here, Paul was responding to a group of sexual ascetics who were apparently demanding that all Christians be celibate. Corinth was the Las Vegas of its day, so that in Greek "being Corinthian" was a verb for being sexually promiscuous. It may have been precisely this environment of excessive sexuality that prompted this one group to want to make celibacy obligatory for Christian life.

2 Paul's view was not that of the ascetics. And yet, it certainly cannot be called a position demonstrating any real appreciation for the intimacy and joy of married life. Some scholars trace this to something in Paul's own experience. If he had once been an observant Jew, then he would have been married, since marriage was one of the commandments. But we meet Paul as unmarried, telling us in this passage that he wished all the Corinthian Christians were celibate like himself. Was his marriage difficult, tragic, disastrous? Had he lost his wife to death or written her off through divorce? Was he a homosexual struggling to live in a heterosexual relationship that never really worked? It's unlikely that we will ever know.

Exactly what was the difference between Paul's position and that of his opponents? Apparently, they required celibacy, while Paul merely preferred it. But, as Paul himself admitted, his support of the option to marry was by way of concession, certainly not command. So Paul walked a middle path between the Jewish view of marriage and family as one of those blessings that should be normative in human experience and the view of the Corinthian faction in which celibacy was the *sine qua non* of a godly life.

Paul set things on an unfortunate path in this regard, and its consequences are all too evident through Christian history, up to and including the sexual disclosures among both Protestant and Catholic clergy in recent years. Lack of sexual understanding on the part of church leaders often hinders their ability to bring a legitimate Christian message to a world hungering for spiritual teaching.

□ Sexual Morality

You have written to me to the effect that it would be better if men avoided sexual intimacy with women completely.[1] But because this could lead to sexual immorality, my advice is that in general men should have wives and women have husbands. By the same token, husbands should have sex with their wives and wives with their husbands. For husbands have authority over their wives' bodies, just as wives have authority over their husbands' bodies. You shouldn't deprive each other, unless this is something you agree to for a limited period of time to dedicate yourselves to prayer. But come together again after these times so that Satan doesn't tempt you because of your inability to control your sexual appetite. Everything I'm writing here is a matter of concession, not of command. Personally, I wish you were all celibate like myself. But each person has his or her own gift from God, and those gifts differ.[2]

—1 Corinthians 7:1–7

1 These words were most probably directed to young people in the community considering getting married or perhaps even already engaged. Paul painted for them a bleak and dismal view of married life as a form of bondage and fleshly troubles. Not one positive word about the joy and encouragement coming from an intimate union was uttered.

2 Paul's largely negative view of marriage and family certainly had something to do with his Hellenistic formation. But his view was also shaped by his apocalyptic mind-set. Scholars often speak of Paul's "provisional ethics" or "interim ethics," meaning that Paul believed that all of our choices must be made against the background of an imminent, world-altering event of cosmic proportions.

Paul described the world much like Pompeii on the day that people were buying and selling, laughing and crying, eating and drinking, loving and hating—while in the distance, the volcano rumbled. The decisions about which people were so concerned—should I buy this or that house or take this or that job—seemed trivial to Paul in terms of the impending judgment.

Paul was wrong in his expectation of a proximate cosmic catastrophe. Nevertheless, reading his words existentially reminds us that the next moment is never a guarantee and that all of our decisions should be made *sub specie aeternitatis,* against the backdrop of eternity. This is surely what Albert Camus meant in saying that we should not ask when judgment day is because it is today.

☐ The Burden of Married Life

I have no ruling from the Lord about the unmarried, but I can give you my own opinion as someone who by God's mercy is reliable. In view of the coming judgment, I think it's best for all of you to remain in the state you're in. If you're bound to a wife, don't seek to be free. If you're free of a wife, don't seek to be bound. You're not sinning if you do decide to marry, whether you're an unmarried man or an unmarried woman. But I'd like to spare you the fleshly troubles experienced by married people.[1] My dear brothers and sisters, the time left to us is short. From now on, even those who have wives should live as though they were single, and those who are in mourning as though they were not in mourning, and those who are celebrating as though they were not celebrating, and those who are buying things as though they were penniless, and those who are doing business with worldly society as though they were not doing business. For the present form of this world is on its way out.[2]

—1 CORINTHIANS 7:25–31

125

1 Because of the vocabulary and the awkwardness of its placement in the text, this passage is an example of verses in Paul's authentic letters interpolated by another hand.

This whole business of male superiority is based here on an interpretation of Genesis 2:21–23. It is often presumed, as in this text, that Adam is male and Eve is made from Adam's rib. But some ancient rabbinic commentators developed a line of thought far less misogynistic. They pointed out that Adam, "the human being," was neither male nor female but androgynous. The word for *rib* can also mean "side," and thus the text can be understood to mean that God divided this androgynous being into two: Adam and Eve, male and female. Male superiority disappears in this alternate interpretation of the text.

Like Jeshu, Paul lived in but resisted the dominant patriarchal culture. His followers were sometimes frightened by Paul's breadth of vision, and they changed his letters or added to them according to their own more limited understanding. For example, Paul ended his Letter to the Romans by greeting Junia (a woman's name) as "prominent among the ambassadors" (Rom. 16:7). But some early copyists changed her feminine name to its masculine form, undoubtedly because they considered it unfitting that a woman should be an ambassador, let alone a prominent one.

☐ Male Superiority

I want you to understand that the head of every man is the Messiah, just as the head of every woman is man, and the head of Christ is God. Any man who prays or speaks in prophecy with covered head disgraces his head, just as any woman who prays or speaks in prophecy with uncovered head disgraces her head—in such a case, she might as well have her head shaved. For if a woman doesn't wear a veil, then she should cut off her hair. But since we all know that it's disgraceful for a woman to cut off her hair or have her head shaved, it's clear that she should wear a veil. A man shouldn't cover his head, since he is the image and glory of God; but a woman is the glory of man. After all, Adam wasn't made from Eve, but Eve from Adam. Nor was Adam created for Eve, but Eve for Adam.[1]

—1 CORINTHIANS 11:3–9

1 Here we have yet another interpolation, a passage that clearly interrupts the flow of the text. Paul was certainly no feminist by today's standards, nor did he demonstrate much insight into the complementary role of the sexes in marriage. But in the context of his time, he clearly supported an active role for women in his communities. In this same letter (16:19), he wrote: "… Aquila and Prisca, together with the community that meets in their house, greet you warmly in the Lord."

In Acts 18:2, we read about Paul meeting this couple, and in Romans 16:3, they are discussed in the most laudatory terms. When the community met in their house, are we to imagine that, even though Paul called both of them his coworkers, only the husband Aquila spoke while Prisca was silent? This contradicts all the evidence for the house churches Paul established, assemblies where Jewish and Gentile Christians, male and female Christians, slave and free Christians, were all called to share their gifts in a spirit of fellowship and peace.

☐ Silence the Women!

As in all of our Christian communities, women should be silent when the community meets. They are not permitted to speak but should be subordinate, as the Torah also teaches us. If there is anything a woman wants to know, she should ask her husband when they get home. For it's disgraceful for a woman to speak in the assembly.[1]

—1 CORINTHIANS 14·34–35

1 Paul argued that Christians were free from observing the dietary rules and other holiness codes that Jews and Judaizers considered binding. And yet, in several places in his letters, as in this passage, he pointed out that having the freedom to do something didn't necessarily mean that doing it was good for one's spiritual life or helpful to others. There is sensitivity and sense in this teaching.

2 Paul taught that our bodies "are members of the Messiah" and are indeed "temples of the Holy Spirit." These are powerful theological affirmations. Unfortunately, Paul developed them only from a negative perspective. He pointed out, for example, that many sins didn't involve our bodies, but some did. But wouldn't it also follow that many of our virtues don't involve our bodies, but some do? Today we might consider some of those: the virtue of not smoking; the virtue of healthy eating and exercise; the virtue of healthy sexual activity.

Sexuality deserved attention both in Paul's time and in ours but once again, instead of illuminating only sexual failings, Paul could have opened the door to a spirituality of blessed participation through honoring the holiness of sex. But given the effect Hellenistic thought had on him, not even counting the hypothesis that his own experiences with sex and marriage were for whatever reason negative, such an expectation might be unrealistic.

Given the distorted sexual attitudes, behaviors, and teachings among Christian leaders today (both Protestant and Catholic), and given the degradation of sexuality in so much of our popular culture, there is all the more urgency for Christian teachers to move us beyond Paul in the recognition and celebration of sexual intimacy and in the encouragement of full gender equality in Christian life and ministry.

☐ Spirituality for Beings with Bodies

I'm allowed to do a lot of things that aren't necessarily helpful. I'm allowed to do a lot of things but I don't want to become addicted to them.[1] Food is for the stomach and the stomach is for food but both will be destroyed by God. The body is not meant for sexual immorality but for the Lord and the Lord is for the body. And God raised the Lord and will raise us by his power too. Don't you know that your bodies are members of the Messiah? Does it make sense then to take the members of the Messiah and make them members of a prostitute? In no way. Don't you know that whoever is united to a prostitute becomes one body with her, for scripture tells us that "the two shall be one flesh"? But anyone united with the Lord becomes one spirit with him. So stay away from sexual immorality. Many of the sins we commit don't directly involve our bodies, but sexual immorality is a sin against the body itself. Don't you realize that your body is a temple of the Holy Spirit in you, the Spirit you have received from God? So you don't really belong to yourself anymore. You were purchased at a high price, so glorify God in your body.[2]

—1 CORINTHIANS 6:12–20

1 In these first verses, Paul clearly devalued and marginalized marriage. This lives on in various ways in Christianity. In the Roman liturgy, for example, saints are categorized as virgins or martyrs, confessors or bishops, but no category exists for the married.

2 Paul reflected the oral tradition, later articulated in the Gospels, that Jeshu took a strong position against divorce, undoubtedly to protect women who were most often the victims of an easy divorce policy. Since a woman's security and survival were tied up with her relationship to a man's house—her father's, her husband's, her married son's—a divorced woman was in an extremely vulnerable position if none of these was available to her.

3 Paul noticed a new situation, one that Jeshu could not have encountered. Conversion to Christianity had led to cases where the non-Christian spouse was unwilling to live with the partner's conversion. This clearly did not lead to the "life of peace" to which Paul claimed we were called.

Consequently, if the non-Christian partner walked out of the relationship, then Paul maintained that the marriage was thereby annulled and the Christian partner was free to remarry. The ruling makes sense and is a good example of Paul's skill in solving problems arising in his communities.

In his development (some might say, contradiction) of Jeshu's clear teaching on divorce, Paul exhibited an unwillingness to be tied rigidly to a tradition, even one that came from Jeshu himself. He thereby demonstrated the need for amending teachings, even sacred teachings, when new situations arose. This attitude stands in sharp contrast to some Christians today who remain persuaded that the answers of the past will always be adequate for the present. Unlike them, Paul regarded sacred teachings and traditions as beginning conversations rather than ending them.

☐ Marriage and Divorce

For single people and widows my advice is to remain unmarried like myself. But if they can't control their sex drives, they should marry. It's better to marry than to constantly be on fire with lust.[1] For those who are married, I have a command—not my own but the Lord's—that the wife should not divorce her husband and the husband should not divorce his wife. If a wife does separate from her husband, she should remain single or find a way to go back to her husband.[2] For others of you I have a ruling (which is mine and does not come from the Lord) that if any Christian man has a non-Christian wife willing to live with him, he should not divorce her. And if any Christian woman has a non-Christian husband willing to live with her, she should not divorce him. For the non-Christian partner is made holy through the Christian partner. But if the non-Christian partner opts to separate, go along with it. In such a case, the Christian partner is no longer bound by the marriage. After all, God calls us to a life of peace.[3]

—1 CORINTHIANS 7:8–15

Love

1 Love for Paul was no mere emotion or sentiment. It was something practical and active, a focused energy that builds up community. Paul linked love with knowledge and good judgment so that good decisions were the result. This is a powerful trinity; any one of these (love, knowledge, judgment) without the other two is dangerous.

2 A pattern of acting according to this rightly guided love produces a life that is "pure and without fault." *Pure* may have meant for Paul focused, centered, one-pointed. It would then correspond to Jeshu's teaching about being "pure of heart" (Matt. 5:8).

It is humanly impossible to be "without fault," but I understand that to mean that whatever failings we have in our past have been brought to the forgiving reality of divine love, a forgiveness that incorporates our past failings into a more God-centered future.

Growing in love, being focused, and having learned from any past failings, we will indeed be ready for whatever comes. Paul was thinking, of course, about the "day of the Messiah," the culminating event of human history. For Christians today who have no expectation of a literal return of Jeshu or a literal judgment, every day is the "day of the Messiah."

3 Lest the Philippians think that they were the ultimate source of right living, Paul reminded them that Jeshu the Messiah was the source of all God-centeredness. The tree bears the apple but only because of the sun, the rain, and the nurturing soil in which the tree is planted.

So, too, they could make good decisions and bear the "fruit of God-centeredness," but only because of the source from which all true life and growth comes, the divine mystery that was their deepest reality. And that source was most fully manifest in the life, teachings, ministry, and faithful death of Jeshu the Messiah.

☐ Love

I pray that your love will keep growing, along with knowledge and discernment, so that you will always recognize the best path.[1] In that way you will be pure and without fault on the day of the Messiah.[2] You will be bearing the fruit of God-centeredness that comes through Jeshu the Messiah for God's praise and glory.[3]

PHILIPPIANS 1:9–11

1 This eloquent passage is only partially true. Virtually all religions have moral codes and holiness codes. This distinction is explained in the introduction. Briefly stated, moral codes involve hurting people, and in the Hebrew Bible, their violation is described as a sin. Paul's examples in this text are all moral codes.

Holiness codes, on the other hand, affect the identity of the community, and their violation is described in the Hebrew Bible as an abomination. In choosing from the Ten Commandments, Paul omitted any holiness codes, such as keeping the Sabbath holy, since that would not support his argument that love fulfilled the Torah. Not keeping the Sabbath doesn't hurt anyone, but it might detract from the community's identity as one that honors a shared day of rest.

Paul's underlying premise was that while the moral codes were eternal, the holiness codes were no longer binding, especially not on Gentile Christians. This enabled him to missionize Gentiles without requiring them to become Jews first. Without this approach, it is unlikely that Christianity would have grown beyond being a Jewish sect. The Judaizers, of course, did not agree with Paul on this point, and it became a major point of disagreement among the early Christians.

It's a moot question today, since Paul's viewpoint prevailed. But it still makes sense for Christians to keep this distinction in mind. After the Second Vatican Council dropped the mandatory abstinence from meat on Fridays (except for the Fridays of Lent), some Catholics wondered whether or not the commandment not to steal might later be dropped as well. Knowing the difference between moral and holiness codes would have helped them answer that question.

Jeshu did not drop the holiness codes, but he clearly subordinated them to the moral codes in such a way that if there was any conflict between the two, the moral code always trumped the holiness code. Thus, Jeshu embraced lepers, even though the holiness codes forbade him to touch them. This can help Christians understand that it's all right to miss attending church on Sunday if such attendance is in conflict with the need to help a neighbor.

☐ Love and Torah Observance

You shouldn't owe anything to anyone except love. When you love someone, you have fulfilled the Torah. The commandments—not to commit adultery, not to murder, not to steal, not to covet, and any other commandment—can all be summed up in one commandment: to love your neighbor as yourself. Since love never wrongs the neighbor, love fulfills the Torah.[1]

—ROMANS 13:8–10

1 Paul's Hellenism emerges in the contrast between the realm of the Flesh and the realm of the Spirit. Notice that the works of the Flesh are not necessarily bodily (e.g., idolatry or sorcery) so much as they are intrinsically disoriented, not God-centered, not Spirit-filled. In other words, the Flesh is a level of consciousness at which some people operate. True freedom cannot be experienced on this fleshly level; only on the spiritual level can human beings know the true nature of freedom.

2 Notice the presumed identity of Flesh and Torah. After three sentences in which he talked about the opposition of Spirit and Flesh, Paul contrasted being led by the Spirit to life under the Torah. Flesh and Torah became synonymous for Paul. Both terms were used by Paul as opposites to Spirit. This is why circumcision, dietary laws, and all Torah-works were at the same level as the vices Paul listed as works of the Flesh. This may explain why physical rituals performed by Christians, such as baptism and Communion, were not works of the Flesh. Though bodily, like circumcision and the dietary laws, they sprang from the Spirit, not from the Flesh.

3 This unjustifiable identity of Torah and Flesh, of Judaism and Torah-works, made it impossible for Paul to enter into any kind of real dialogue with Judaism. And this bias continued into Christian history, so that many Christians to this day speak of Judaism as a religion of works, a fleshly religion, and Christianity as a religion of faith, a spiritual religion. A thorough reeducation to the truth and spiritual validity of Judaism is incumbent on any Christian desiring to get past the limitations of Paul's views on this matter.

☐ The Flesh Does Not Do the Works of Love

Live your lives in the Spirit so that you won't end up caught in the impulses of the Flesh. For the Flesh opposes the Spirit just as the Spirit opposes the Flesh. These two are antagonistic to each other, and the result is that you aren't able to do the things you want to do.[1] But if you're led by the Spirit, you're not under the Torah.[2] Now the works of the Flesh are clear enough: fornication, immorality, debauchery, idolatry, sorcery, grudges, strife, enmity, anger, quarrels, dissensions, factions, jealousy, drunkenness, carousing, and other things of this kind. I warn you now, as I warned you before, that those who exhibit this kind of behavior will not inherit God's Kingdom.[3]

—GALATIANS 5:16–23

1 Paul's past life in Judaism was in some sense bondage, just as his new life in Jeshu the Messiah was in a very real sense freedom. Paul generalized his experience of his former faith (trusting the covenant with God made at Sinai) and came to consider all of his fellow religionists not sharing his new faith (trusting the covenant with God made through the Messiah) as still in bondage. Thus, everything Jewish was by definition of the Flesh.

I capitalize *Flesh* in these translations to show that it represents a state of understanding the world (consciousness) and living in the world (conscience). The Flesh is not synonymous with the body. Bodily activities can glorify God; the Flesh cannot. Fleshly living revolves around our false selves, unaware of any need to love God or neighbor. The Flesh is closed to the call to serve others in love.

Paul's communities were "called to freedom." He considered them to be of the Spirit, not of the Flesh. Thus, in Paul's theology, the "old covenant" and everything pertaining to it was fleshly, while the "new covenant" and everything pertaining to it was spiritual. True freedom, for Paul, was also spiritual. And this freedom could only be enjoyed by those sharing the faith of his communities. It was only those community members, according to Paul, who could enjoy freedom, who could truly love, and who could rightly claim to be God's sons and daughters.

2 Nevertheless, even the members of Paul's communities could sin. They could deviate from the paths of the Spirit and follow the ways of the Flesh. How were they to know the difference? The criterion was love. This is not romantic sentiment but sincerely willing the good of the neighbor, acting effectively to help the neighbor, creating the kind of community in which the neighbor can grow.

☐ Love Needs Freedom

My brothers and sisters, you are being called to freedom. Make sure that
you don't use this freedom as license for the Flesh.[1] Serve one another in
love. For the entire Torah can be understood in this one command: Love
your neighbor as yourself.[2]

—GALATIANS 5:13–14

1 Love, for Paul, was the radiating center of community life. This love was no mere emotional high, something subject to the vagaries of passing feelings and fancies. True love entailed a commitment to building community through a consistent, positive regard for the community members, leading to effective action on their behalf.

Many centuries after this text was written, Thomas Aquinas would say: *Amor est velle bonum alterius.* "Love means willing the good of another." We notice that Aquinas, like Paul, placed love in the will, not in the emotions. Love must aim at results. Effectively willing the good of the other means doing what we can to achieve that good. Jeshu himself taught that we know a tree by its fruit (Matt. 7:17).

2 In this paragraph we see the diminution of the false self as a prerequisite for any growth in love. All the negative traits in this passage stem from overinflated egos, and all the positive traits follow from an ability truly to be open to the other and value the other fully.

3 Love lasts and lasts and lasts, beyond anything else we will ever know. This sheer willing of the good has no limits, no boundaries, and no end. Faith ends when we experience what we have trusted; hope ends when we attain what we had hoped for; but love continues without any change in its essential nature.

□ The Greatest Gift

If I master all the languages that humans and angels speak but don't have love, I'm just a noisy gong or clanging piece of metal. And if I am a super prophet, understanding all mysteries and possessing all knowledge, with mountain-moving faith, but without love, I am nothing. If I give away everything and even boast about surrendering myself to my enemies, but don't have love, I have nothing.[1] Love is patient and kind, never jealous, bragging, arrogant, or rude. It doesn't demand its own way, is not irritable or resentful, doesn't enjoy it when others are wrong but enjoys whatever is right. Love of this sort is ready to put up with everything, believe everything, hope for everything, persevere through everything.[2] Love never comes to an end. Prophecies do, as well as speaking in tongues and knowledge. For what we know is partial and what we say in prophecy is partial; but when what is complete comes, everything partial will be over. When I was a child, I talked, thought, and reasoned like a child; but as an adult, I have dropped these childish ways. Now I know only partially, but in the end I will know fully, even as I have been fully known. For now faith, hope, and love remain, all three; but what is most important is love.[3]

—1 CORINTHIANS 13:1–13

The End Times

1 *Parousia* is the Greek word for the triumphal entrance of a conquering general into his home city. It is what we might call a ticker tape parade, and it is the underlying metaphor in this passage. Jeshu lived in poverty and died in the humiliation of a public execution, but he will return to earth and his "second coming" (a phrase never used in the Christian Testament) will be in glory, as a victor.

Paul presumed that he and most of his fellow Christians would be alive when Jeshu returned. In a secular *parousia*, people would run out to meet the conquering general as he approached the city and then accompany him into the city. Current popular understandings of this event (for example, that God "raptures" the true believers and takes them to heaven) fail to grasp the underlying metaphor of *parousia*. The faithful (both those who had died and were raised and those still alive) are not caught up (*rapti* is the Latin word, thus *rapture*) to go to heaven but to accompany the Lord as he enters the city (that is, comes to reign on earth).

Most scholars today do not understand this symbolic language literally. No one is coming on the clouds; nor will there be trumpet blasts or angelic voices. These are poetic ways of describing God's ultimate victory. When humanity evolves to its fullest spiritual potential, then Christ's *parousia* will have taken place. This prophecy is beautifully described in Jeremiah 31:34: "No longer shall they teach one another, or say to one another, 'Know the Lord,' for they shall all know me, from the least of them to the greatest."

This extraordinary verse from Jeremiah foresees a time when all dualism is transcended. No one has to teach anyone else to know God, for that knowledge will reside in every human heart. It is important to remember here that the Hebrew word for *know* also means to have sexual intercourse. In the Hebrew language, knowledge does not live above the eyebrows; it is experienced intimacy.

The verse thus foretells a time when all of humankind will live and operate at a level of mystical consciousness. Meanwhile, although that stage of planetary evolution still lies in the future, an individual manifesting what in Christian language is called "Christ consciousness" becomes an *alter Christus*, another Christ. And without clouds or trumpets, Jeshu the Messiah has already returned in that person.

☐ Christ's Return

My dear brothers and sisters, I don't want you to have the wrong idea about those among you who have passed on, so that you end up grieving like those who have no hope for life beyond the grave. If Jeshu died and rose again, as we believe, then through Jeshu, God will bring with him those who have passed on. I'm telling you this now as God's word: those of us who are still alive, left on earth until the Lord's coming in triumph, will not be taken up ahead of those who have passed on. For the Lord himself, with the commanding voice of a conqueror, accompanied by the archangel's shout and the blast of God's trumpet, will descend from heaven; and it is those who have passed on in the Messiah who will rise first. Then those of us who are alive, who still remain on earth, will be caught up in the clouds, along with the others, to meet the Lord in the air. And so it is that we will be with the Lord forever.[1]

—1 THESSALONIANS 4:13–17

1 This simile ("at night like a thief") has an interesting history. Quite possibly the earliest use of this image, the one closest to the words of Jeshu himself, can be found in the Gospel of Thomas, saying 21B. There we are told to guard ourselves against the world coming at night like a thief to rob us.

The world in this case refers to what we call worldliness, an orientation closed to God's reign. This worldliness can creep in on us unexpectedly and rob us of our true treasure, our God-centeredness. We need to be alert and watchful, looking for all those subtle and not so subtle ways in which we change our allegiance from God's reign to Caesar's reign, another image for "the world."

But in this text of Paul, the metaphor has shifted its meaning and refers to the end times. This is parallel to what we find in Matthew 24:42–43 and Luke 12:39–40, where it is the Son of Man who is coming like a thief in the night. And yet, it makes better poetic (and theological) sense to understand the thief as worldliness, something negative, rather than as either Jeshu or his return.

The underlying question, of course, is whether Jeshu's view was apocalyptic at all. In other words, was his message oriented to a future inbreaking action of God? I am persuaded by those scholars who say no, maintaining that Jeshu focused on the present moment and had no particular message regarding the end of the present world order. Paul and some other early Christians, on the other hand, clearly did.

But if Paul was wrong in his apocalyptic expectations, at least he did not fall into the trap of some later Christians and try to work out a timetable of these end-time events. Nevertheless, we might do well to return to the saying as we find it in the Gospel of Thomas. Worldliness is a real and present danger. A surreptitiously returning Jeshu is not.

☐ Christ Will Come Again

My dear brothers and sisters, there's no need for me to give you some kind of calendar for these end-time events. For you know very well that the day of the Lord will come at night like a thief.[1]

—1 THESSALONIANS 5:1–2

1 Jeshu models the future of all the faithful. Because he has been raised from the dead, they will be raised as well; but if he has not been raised from the dead, then they face nothing more than the absurdity of total extinction.

2 The resurrection of Jeshu—and the promised resurrection of all the faithful—was central to Paul's message. Without this central plank, Paul's platform would collapse.

3 Paul taught that the death and resurrection of Jeshu offered believers the forgiveness of their sins. Forgiveness always provides future, an invitation to move forward beyond the limitations of past failings. But if Jeshu has not been raised from the dead, then the faithful remain mired in their sins with nothing to call them into a future.

4 The underlying question here is the nature of resurrection, both Jeshu's and the believer's. Is this a physical resuscitation or is this a spiritual transformation? Paul addressed this question in some of the later passages in this chapter.

☐ Death and Resurrection

Since we've announced the Messiah as raised from the dead, how can some of you deny the resurrection of the dead?[1] If there's no resurrection of the dead, then neither has the Messiah been raised from the dead. But if the Messiah has not been raised from the dead, then what we've been announcing is meaningless, as is your faith.[2] We're even exposed as false witnesses for God, claiming that God has raised the Messiah from the dead, since if the dead are not raised, then neither is the Messiah. And if the Messiah has not been raised from the dead, then your faith is meaningless and you are still in your sins.[3] And that means that those who have fallen asleep in the Messiah have perished. If our hope in the Messiah is only for this life, then we are the most pitiful people of all.[4]

—1 CORINTHIANS 15:12–19

1 Paul foresaw an imminent end to the present world order. This was one of the chief factors driving his mission. He was, of course, wrong. And we have no way of knowing how Paul would have changed if he had come to realize that he was wrong about something so fundamental to his worldview.

But if Paul was wrong about the end of the present world order in his lifetime, what else was he wrong about? And if he was indeed receiving revelations from God, why didn't God correct this fundamental error? My response is that an authentic mystical relationship to God (which Christians certainly believe Paul had) does not alter all of a person's socialized limitations. Why else does no author of any of the books either in the Hebrew Bible or in the Christian Testament condemn slavery?

So we can take what Paul had to say and allow it to live through the subsequent years of human experience, bringing it up to our own day. Much of what he said was timeless, and the urgency he felt can readily be transformed from a temporal to an existential mode. Today may indeed be the last day of my life or of human life as we know it, and it makes sense to live life from that perspective.

2 Although Paul was not entirely consistent on this point, Flesh and body were usually not synonymous for him. We have seen passages where Paul talked about glorifying God in our bodies. The Flesh meant for Paul a lower level of consciousness, a darkened mind from which flowed "the works of darkness."

The Flesh further signified for Paul the whole present state of humanity, except for those few who had come to daylight through their faith in Jeshu the Messiah. This is why Judaism, without faith in Jeshu the Messiah, was fleshly for Paul. Christians, however, as new creations, were called to embody a life of higher consciousness, one that would be revealed to the whole world when Jeshu the Messiah returned.

☐ Imminent Second Coming

Believe me when I say that this is a critical time. It's time to wake up. Salvation is a lot closer than when we first became believers. The night is almost over and the day is dawning.[1] It's time to put aside the works of darkness and put on the armor of light. We should live honorably, as people do in daylight. This is not the time for the activities of the night: drunken parties, sex orgies, and brawls. It's time to stop pandering to fleshly desires and put on the Lord Jeshu the Messiah.[2]

—ROMANS 13:11–14

1 Some Jews and Christians to this day believe that resurrection entails a resuscitation of our current bodies. Thus, they may forbid cremation or even organ transplants. They believe that it is indeed this body, the one we see in the mirror, that is going to heaven. Paul's Hellenism would not allow him to accept this idea. The risen body could not be the corruptible body that we experience. To be corruptible meant to be subject to decay. Something subject to decay couldn't enter heaven.

But as a Jew, Paul believed, like the Pharisees, that our future life must somehow be bodily, since in Hebrew language and thought we are holistic beings, incapable of being separated into body and soul entities. Living between two ways of thinking, how could Paul resolve this dilemma?

2 *Mystery* has the same root (*mu*, "to be silent") as *myth* and *mystic*. These words take us beyond the world of factuality to one explicable only in poetic language. Struggling with the conflicting views of Judaism and Hellenism, Paul moved beyond factual description to the language of mystery. Life after death necessitated a spiritual body. Here was a concept that satisfied both his Jewish soul and his Hellenistic mind.

3 The old Latin liturgy had a beautiful phrase describing the transition from our present life to the next: *Vita mutatur non tollitur*. "Life is changed, not taken away." The statement is modest in refraining from trying to say what cannot be said. It respects the poetic language Paul used in passages like this.

4 The tragic anti-Jewishness in this verse is consistent with Paul's view that the Torah without Jeshu the Messiah no longer represented a valid covenantal relationship with God and was, therefore, a revelation of sin without the power to forgive sin.

5 The realization that death is the opposite of birth, not of life, robs death of its vaunted finality. The transitional character of death is affirmed in virtually all the great sacred traditions. The metaphors differ—resurrection, reincarnation, going to heaven—but the basic affirmation of the ongoingness of life is present in each.

☐ Resurrection as Transformation

I want you to know, my brothers and sisters, that flesh and blood cannot inherit God's reign nor can corruptible things inherit what is incorruptible.[1] Pay attention and I will tell you a mystery.[2] We will not all fall asleep in death, but we will all be changed in a moment, in the blink of an eye, with the last trumpet.[3] For it is with the sound of that trumpet that we will be changed and the dead will be raised incorruptible. For the corruptible body must put on incorruptibility and the mortal body must put on immortality. When this corruptible body puts on incorruptibility and this mortal body puts on immortality, then the word of scripture will be fulfilled: Death has been swallowed up in victory. Where is death's victory and where is death's sting? Death's sting is sin and sin's power is the Torah.[4] Thank God that we've been given a victory over death and sin through our Lord Jeshu the Messiah.[5]

—1 CORINTHIANS 15:50–57

1 Paul branded as foolishness any attempts to understand resurrection (whether Jeshu's or that of his fellow Christians) in a literal way. Paul was leading his readers to a realm of symbolic understanding where they could grasp that the mystery of resurrection is not about a mere resuscitation of the body that is put in the ground and buried.

2 When we plant our gardens, we notice the difference between the little black seeds in our hand and the green heads of lettuce pictured on the envelopes in which the seeds come. We don't plant little black seeds with the hope of harvesting big black seeds. We harvest beautiful heads of lettuce bearing little resemblance to little black seeds.

3 The insight Paul was leading his readers to was that the resurrected body was a spiritual body, as unlike the physical body that was buried as the head of lettuce is unlike the little black seed that was planted. But what is a spiritual body? Is that not an oxymoron?

The body is essential to our identity. And yet, the identity we have as resurrected beings in God is not like the identity we have now. Resurrection is a spiritual reality, and the resurrected body is spiritual as well. It is transformation-with-identity that is central here, not literal, cell-for-cell identity.

□ A Spiritual Body

Some of you are asking how the dead are raised and what kind of body those raised from the dead will have. Don't be foolish.[1] The seeds you plant in the ground don't come to life until they die. And what you plant doesn't look like what you will harvest. You put a bare seed in the ground, perhaps of wheat or some other grain. God gives it the form it will have when you harvest it, and each kind of seed is given a different kind of form.[2] Human beings, animals, birds, and fish all have different kinds of bodies. There are heavenly bodies and earthly bodies, and the glory of the former differs from the glory of the latter. The sun has one kind of glory and the moon and the stars another. Why, even one star differs from another star in glory. It's the same with the resurrection of the dead. What we bury is perishable; what is raised cannot perish. What we bury is without glory; what is raised is glorious. What we bury cannot even move anymore; what is raised is powerful. What we bury is a physical body; what is raised is a spiritual body. If there is a physical body, there must be a spiritual body too.[3]

—1 CORINTHIANS 15:35–44

1 Life is difficult. It was difficult for Paul, and it's difficult for us. That's the First Noble Truth of Buddhism, one that doesn't require much defense. Paul's expectation of an imminent end to the present order of the world provided him with consolation in the midst of life's difficulties.

But what consoles those contemporary Christians who see no evidence, biblical or otherwise, for expecting an imminent end time? What else but the experience of God's reign and the presence of God's Spirit in the present moment? Living in the Spirit, living in the holiness of the here and now, experiencing God's peace now, tasting heaven (the Eternal Now) in the miracle of this moment—these are the consolations of a God-centered life.

2 Material creation is personified as though it were a living being longing for the glorious transformation that is the future of the human community. Just as the material world is damaged by human sin, so too will it be restored by human transformation. In Paul's view, everything and everyone has an innate longing to grow beyond this present era in which sin, ignorance, and death are so dominant. The world wants to "grow up," and so do we. But with so little evidence of such growth in sight, whether in Paul's world or in ours, we try to be steadfast in hope and practiced in patience. Nevertheless, a God-centered life, a life open to God's reign, allows us to enjoy repeated glimpses into the glory awaiting those whose hearts are God-centered.

☐ This Age and the Age to Come

As far as I'm concerned, the hardships we experience now pale by comparison with the glory that is going to be revealed in us.[1] The material world of creation consumes itself with longing for the glorious, end-time revelation of God's children. Purposelessness infected the material world of creation, not because of anything in itself but because of Adam's sin. But this very sin gives birth to the hope that the material world of creation will eventually be free from its present bondage to decay and will be brought to the glorious freedom of God's children. Up to this present time, the whole material world of creation has been like a woman crying out in labor. And it's not only the material world of creation but we ourselves, who have the Spirit as a foretaste of glory; we too cry inwardly while we wait for the transformation of our bodily existence. For we were saved by our hope. You don't hope for something that you already have. Who would hope for something right there in front of them? But if we hope for what we don't have in front of us, we patiently wait for it.[2]

—ROMANS 8:18–25

God's Plan for the Jews

1 Even in such passionate expressions of loyalty and love we can detect Paul's Hellenistic mind-set. The Jews were his family "in the Flesh." But as we see in other passages, the Flesh cannot know God. His fellow Christians, however, were his family in the Spirit. Only the Spirit and those who live in the Spirit can know God. All the advantages Jews had through their history would be nullified if they did not come to faith in Jeshu the Messiah.

2 The Messiah, like Paul, was a Jew "according to the Flesh." But such fleshly identity carried no real value. For Paul, it was only spiritual identity that determined salvation or damnation. So even though Paul's primary mission was to the Gentiles, he never lost sight of God's plan for his fellow Jews. They too could know eternal life only through their faith in Jeshu the Messiah.

3 The passage ends with the sweeping cadences of a hymn. It even has a closing "Amen." There is an ambiguity in the Greek phrasing of this final sentence. It could be translated as "he is God over all, blessed forever" or (as in this translation) "he is over all, blessed be God forever." I prefer this latter translation because the identification of Jeshu the Messiah with God (*theos*) occurs nowhere else in Paul's authentic letters. When Paul talked about God (*theos*), he was inevitably referring to "the Father."

What's the significance of this? Was Jeshu divine because he was a different kind of being than the rest of us? Was he indeed a heavenly being who came to earth? Or was Jeshu divine because he was like all of us—made in God's image, only more fully so? In that case, he was different from us not in kind but in the degree to which he manifested the divine reality existing in everyone and everything.

Paul's ideas about the Messiah provided a basis for a later doctrine of the Trinity. God was one, but Christians experienced God as Father, as manifested in Jeshu, and as known in the life of the Spirit within us. The Greek and Latin words for *person* suggested the mask used by an actor. The one God wore three masks. Or, just as I am son to my father, brother to my brother, and father to my son, so too can we know God in three ways.

☐ Paul's Love for His People

I would be willing to be damned and separated from the Messiah if that could in any way help my own people, my family in the Flesh.[1] They are Israelites. Divine adoption, God's glory, the covenants, the giving of the Torah, the sacred liturgy, and the promises all belong to them. The patriarchs are their patriarchs and it's from them that the Messiah comes, according to the Flesh,[2] and he is over all, blessed be God forever. Amen.[3]

—ROMANS 9:3–5

1 Paul obviously had a problem. His fellow Jews, for the most part, rejected his message of Jeshu as Messiah; and yet, many Gentiles responded positively to this same message. How could that be? Paul could not accept God's final rejection of Israel. He loved his fellow Jews too much to believe that was possible.

God must have another plan in mind. Perhaps Israel's rejection was making room for the inclusion of Gentiles, thus helping Paul's mission to the Gentiles. The Jews would eventually become jealous when they saw that so many Gentiles had found God-centeredness through faith in Jeshu the Messiah, and they would be prompted to join the community of Christian believers.

That was Paul's hope. Some Christians today still cling to the belief that a future mass conversion of Jews will be part of the events associated with the Messiah's end-time return. But most contemporary Christians realize that Paul's attempted explanations were based on an exclusivist theology they do not share.

An alternate response to Paul's dilemma would be the recognition that Jews continue to find God-centeredness through their faith in the revelation at Sinai, just as Christians find God-centeredness through their faith in what was revealed in Jeshu. From this perspective, no one was rejected, and what Paul saw as Jewish stubbornness and stumbling was actually Jewish faithfulness to their own covenantal relationship to God.

☐ Jews Will Be Saved

Has God rejected his people? Of course not. I myself am an Israelite, Abraham's descendant, of Benjamin's tribe. This is the people God knew before they ever existed. There's no way God could reject them.... So I have to ask if they are rejected because they have stumbled. Not at all. It's because of their stumbling that salvation has come to the Gentiles, and the calling of the Gentiles to faith should make Israel jealous. If their stumbling enriched the world and if their defeat enriched the Gentiles, how much more important will their inclusion mean?[1]

—ROMANS 11:1–2; 11–12

1 Paul was speaking to the largely Gentile Christian community in Rome. Noticing that so few Jews accepted Jeshu as Messiah, it might well be that the Gentile Christians there began to feel superior to the Jewish unbelievers. Paul wanted them to remain humble, gratefully remembering that the Jewish rejection made room for them.

But why was one group's rejection necessary for another group's inclusion? It may be that Paul had an idea that a set number of souls was destined to be saved so that one dropping out made room for someone else.

2 Paul developed a metaphor of the olive tree and its branches. If the tree represented the whole history of faithful Israel, from Abraham's time to Paul's, then the Jews who accepted Jeshu as Messiah represented faithful Israel in these end times, just as the Jews who rejected Jeshu as Messiah represented faithless Israel.

3 The faithless Jews were like branches lopped off the tree, and faithful Gentiles could then be grafted on in their place. But Paul admonished these Gentile Christians not to feel boastful about their new place of honor. For if they proved not faithful, God would certainly cut them off, just as God cut off the faithless Jews.

Perhaps Paul's letter caused the Gentile Christians in Rome to be more humble in the realization that some Jews "gave up their seats" so that they could be saved. And yet, in the long run, Paul's exclusivism created more of the very arrogance he wanted to correct.

For whenever a group of people believes that it alone has the truth, it is difficult for those people to avoid either religious pride or the presumed right to proselytize others. And that, unfortunately, is the story of much of Christianity's subsequent history. It is the background to every crusade and inquisition, every pogrom and persecution. And it explains why, even today, street-corner evangelists or televangelists all believe that they know your religious truth better than you do.

☐ Gentile Christians Should Be Humble

I want to speak now to those in the community who are Gentile Christians. I am, after all, an apostle to the Gentiles, and I'm proud to call Gentiles to salvation partly because it might make my own people jealous and in that way some of them may be saved too.[1] Because if their current rejection of faith is helping the rest of the world to find its way to God, then their acceptance of faith will be nothing less than life from the dead. If the bit of dough offered as a first-fruit offering is holy, then so too is the whole batch; and if the root is holy, then so too are the branches. Now if some of the branches were cut off and you, a wild olive branch, were grafted on in their place to share in the richness of the olive tree's roots, don't brag about being superior to the branches.[2] If you are tempted to brag, remember that you're not the ones nourishing the roots, but rather it's the roots that are nourishing you. You may well claim that branches were cut off so that you could be grafted on. That's all well and good. They were cut off because of their lack of faith, just as you are there only because of your faith. So don't be proud but have a healthy fear. For if God didn't spare the natural branches, perhaps he will not spare you either.[3]

—ROMANS 11:13–22

Suggestions for Further Reading ☐

Bornkamm, Günther. *Paul*. New York: Harper & Row, 1971.

Boyarin, Daniel. *A Radical Jew: Paul and the Politics of Identity*. Berkeley: University of California Press, 1994.

Crossan, John D., and Jonathan L. Reed. *In Search of Paul: How Jesus's Apostle Opposed Rome's Empire with God's Kingdom*. San Francisco: HarperSanFrancisco, 2004.

Gager, John G. *Reinventing Paul*. Oxford: Oxford University Press, 2000.

Hengel, Martin. *Between Jesus and Paul*. Philadelphia: Fortress Press, 1983.

Maccoby, Hyam. *The Mythmaker: Paul and the Invention of Christianity*. New York: Barnes & Noble Books, 1986.

Miller, Ron. *The Gospel of Thomas: A Guidebook for Spiritual Practice*. Woodstock, VT: SkyLight Paths, 2004.

———. *The Hidden Gospel of Matthew: Annotated and Explained*. Woodstock, VT: SkyLight Paths, 2004.

Miller, Ron, and Laura Bernstein. *Healing the Jewish-Christian Rift: Growing Beyond Our Wounded History*. Woodstock, VT: SkyLight Paths, 2006.

Murphy-O'Connor, Jerome. *Paul: A Critical Life*. Oxford: Oxford University Press, 1997.

Pagels, Elaine. *The Gnostic Paul: Gnostic Exegesis of the Pauline Letters*. Philadelphia: Trinity Press International, 1975.

Sanders, E. P. *Paul, the Law, and the Jewish People*. Philadelphia: Fortress Press, 1983.

Index of Bible Passages Annotated ☐

Romans

1:18–20	27
2:12–13	101
2:25–29	117
3:9–10	109
3:20	99
3:22B–26	29
4:9B–12	31
5:12–14	39
5:17–19	41
6:1–7	21
6:12–14	23
7:14–20	19
8:18–25	161
8:28–31	81
8:32–39	83
9:3–5	165
9:30–32A	115
10:9–13	33
11:1–2; 11–12	167
11:13–22	169
12:2	47
12:9–18	55
13:1–7	59
13:8–10	139
13:11–14	155

1 Corinthians

1:18–25	113
2:6–7	11
5:9–13	69
6:9–11	71
6:12–20	131
7:1–7	123
7:8–15	133
7:25–31	125
10:12–13	25
10:16–17	91
10:23–31	77
11:3–9	127
11:20–22	93
11:23–26	95
12:4–11	57
12:12–18	75
12:27–31	73
13:1–13	145
14:34–35	129
15:3–10	7
15:12–19	153
15:20–28	43
15:35–44	159
15:50–57	157

2 Corinthians

1:3–7	67
3:1–3	65
3:4–6	13
3:12–16	119
5:16–17	37
11:21–28	9
12:1–10	15

Galatians

1:1–5	3
2:1–9	5
2:11–14	103
2:19–20	107
3:10–14	111
3:23–28	105
5:13–14	143
5:16–23	141
6:7–9	79

Philippians

1:9–11	137
2:1–4	49
2:5–11	85
4:4–7	53
4:8–9	51

1 Thessalonians

4:9–12	61
4:13–17	149
5:1–2	151
5:14–22	63

Philemon

1:10–16	87

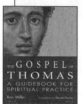

Spirituality of the Seasons

Autumn: A Spiritual Biography of the Season
Edited by Gary Schmidt and Susan M. Felch; Illustrations by Mary Azarian
Rejoice in autumn as a time of preparation and reflection. Includes Wendell Berry, David James Duncan, Robert Frost, A. Bartlett Giamatti, E. B. White, P. D. James, Julian of Norwich, Garret Keizer, Tracy Kidder, Anne Lamott, May Sarton.
6 x 9, 320 pp, 5 b/w illus., Quality PB, 978-1-59473-118-1 **$18.99**
HC, 978-1-59473-005-4 **$22.99**

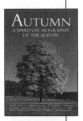

Spring: A Spiritual Biography of the Season
Edited by Gary Schmidt and Susan M. Felch; Illustrations by Mary Azarian
Explore the gentle unfurling of spring and reflect on how nature celebrates rebirth and renewal. Includes Jane Kenyon, Lucy Larcom, Harry Thurston, Nathaniel Hawthorne, Noel Perrin, Annie Dillard, Martha Ballard, Barbara Kingsolver, Dorothy Wordsworth, Donald Hall, David Brill, Lionel Basney, Isak Dinesen, Paul Laurence Dunbar.
6 x 9, 352 pp, 6 b/w illus., HC, 978-1-59473-114-3 **$21.99**

Summer: A Spiritual Biography of the Season
Edited by Gary Schmidt and Susan M. Felch; Illustrations by Barry Moser
"A sumptuous banquet…. These selections lift up an exquisite wholeness found within an everyday sophistication."— ★ *Publishers Weekly* starred review
Includes Anne Lamott, Luci Shaw, Ray Bradbury, Richard Selzer, Thomas Lynch, Walt Whitman, Carl Sandburg, Sherman Alexie, Madeleine L'Engle, Jamaica Kincaid.
6 x 9, 304 pp, 5 b/w illus., HC, 978-1-59473-083-2 **$21.99**

Winter: A Spiritual Biography of the Season
Edited by Gary Schmidt and Susan M. Felch; Illustrations by Barry Moser
"This outstanding anthology features top-flight nature and spirituality writers on the fierce, inexorable season of winter…. Remarkably lively and warm, despite the icy subject." — ★ *Publishers Weekly* starred review.
Includes Will Campbell, Rachel Carson, Annie Dillard, Donald Hall, Ron Hansen, Jane Kenyon, Jamaica Kincaid, Barry Lopez, Kathleen Norris, John Updike, E. B. White.
6 x 9, 288 pp, 6 b/w illus., Deluxe PB w/flaps, 978-1-893361-92-8 **$18.95**
HC, 978-1-893361-53-9 **$21.95**

Spirituality / Animal Companions

Blessing the Animals: Prayers and Ceremonies to Celebrate God's Creatures, Wild and Tame   *Edited by Lynn L. Caruso* 5 x 7¼, 256 pp, HC, 978-1-59473-145-7 **$19.99**

What Animals Can Teach Us about Spirituality: Inspiring Lessons from Wild and Tame Creatures   *by Diana L. Guerrero* 6 x 9, 176 pp, Quality PB, 978-1-893361-84-3 **$16.95**

Spirituality

Awakening the Spirit, Inspiring the Soul
30 Stories of Interspiritual Discovery in the Community of Faiths
Edited by Brother Wayne Teasdale and Martha Howard, MD; Foreword by Joan Borysenko, PhD
Thirty original spiritual mini-autobiographies showcase the varied ways that people come to faith—and what that means—in today's multi-religious world.
6 x 9, 224 pp, HC, 978-1-59473-039-9 **$21.99**

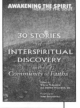

The Alphabet of Paradise: An A–Z of Spirituality for Everyday Life
by Howard Cooper 5 x 7¾, 224 pp, Quality PB, 978-1-893361-80-5 **$16.95**

Creating a Spiritual Retirement: A Guide to the Unseen Possibilities in Our Lives
by Molly Srode 6 x 9, 208 pp, b/w photos, Quality PB, 978-1-59473-050-4 **$14.99**
HC, 978-1-893361-75-1 **$19.95**

Finding Hope: Cultivating God's Gift of a Hopeful Spirit
by Marcia Ford 8 x 8, 200 pp, Quality PB, 978-1-59473-211-9 **$16.99**

The Geography of Faith: Underground Conversations on Religious, Political and Social Change   *by Daniel Berrigan and Robert Coles* 6 x 9, 224 pp, Quality PB, 978-1-893361-40-9 **$16.95**

God Within: Our Spiritual Future—As Told by Today's New Adults   *Edited by Jon M. Sweeney and the Editors at SkyLight Paths* 6 x 9, 176 pp, Quality PB, 978-1-893361-15-7 **$14.95**

Sacred Texts—SkyLight Illuminations Series

Offers today's spiritual seeker an accessible entry into the great classic texts of the world's spiritual traditions. Each classic is presented in an accessible translation, with facing pages of guided commentary from experts, giving you the keys you need to understand the history, context and meaning of the text. This series enables you, whatever your background, to experience and understand classic spiritual texts directly, and to make them a part of your life.

CHRISTIANITY

The End of Days: Essential Selections from Apocalyptic Texts—
Annotated & Explained *Annotation by Robert G. Clouse*
Helps you understand the complex Christian visions of the end of the world.
5½ x 8½, 224 pp, Quality PB, 978-1-59473-170-9 **$16.99**

The Hidden Gospel of Matthew: Annotated & Explained
Translation & Annotation by Ron Miller
Takes you deep into the text cherished around the world to discover the words and events that have the strongest connection to the historical Jesus.
5½ x 8½, 272 pp, Quality PB, 978-1-59473-038-2 **$16.99**

The Lost Sayings of Jesus: Teachings from Ancient Christian, Jewish, Gnostic and Islamic Sources—Annotated & Explained
Translation & Annotation by Andrew Phillip Smith; Foreword by Stephan A. Hoeller
This collection of more than three hundred sayings depicts Jesus as a Wisdom teacher who speaks to people of all faiths as a mystic and spiritual master.
5½ x 8½, 240 pp, Quality PB, 978-1-59473-172-3 **$16.99**

Philokalia: The Eastern Christian Spiritual Texts—Selections Annotated & Explained *Annotation by Allyne Smith; Translation by G. E. H. Palmer, Phillip Sherrard and Bishop Kallistos Ware*
The first approachable introduction to the wisdom of the Philokalia, which is the classic text of Eastern Christian spirituality.
5½ x 8½, 240 pp, Quality PB, 978-1-59473-103-7 **$16.99**

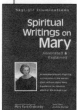

Spiritual Writings on Mary: Annotated & Explained
Annotation by Mary Ford-Grabowsky; Foreword by Andrew Harvey
Examines the role of Mary, the mother of Jesus, as a source of inspiration in history and in life today. 5½ x 8½, 288 pp, Quality PB, 978-1-59473-001-6 **$16.99**

The Way of a Pilgrim: Annotated & Explained
Translation & Annotation by Gleb Pokrovsky; Foreword by Andrew Harvey
This classic of Russian spirituality is the delightful account of one man who sets out to learn the prayer of the heart, also known as the "Jesus prayer."
5½ x 8½, 160 pp, Illus., Quality PB, 978-1-893361-31-7 **$14.95**

MORMONISM

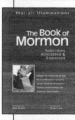

The Book of Mormon: Selections Annotated & Explained
Annotation by Jana Riess; Foreword by Phyllis Tickle
Explores the sacred epic that is cherished by more than twelve million members of the LDS church as the keystone of their faith.
5½ x 8½ , 272 pp, Quality PB, 978-1-59473-076-4 **$16.99**

NATIVE AMERICAN

Native American Stories of the Sacred: Annotated & Explained
Retold & Annotated by Evan T. Pritchard
Intended for more than entertainment, these teaching tales contain elegantly simple illustrations of time-honored truths.
5½ x 8½, 272 pp, Quality PB, 978-1-59473-112-9 **$16.99**

Sacred Texts—cont.

GNOSTICISM

The Gospel of Philip: Annotated & Explained
Translation & Annotation by Andrew Phillip Smith; Foreword by Stevan Davies
Reveals otherwise unrecorded sayings of Jesus and fragments of Gnostic mythology.
5½ x 8½, 160 pp, Quality PB, 978-1-59473-111-2 **$16.99**

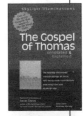

The Gospel of Thomas: Annotated & Explained
Translation & Annotation by Stevan Davies Sheds new light on the origins of Christianity and
portrays Jesus as a wisdom-loving sage. 5½ x 8½, 192 pp, Quality PB, 978-1-893361-45-4 **$16.99**

The Secret Book of John: The Gnostic Gospel—Annotated & Explained
Translation & Annotation by Stevan Davies The most significant and influential text of
the ancient Gnostic religion. 5½ x 8½, 208 pp, Quality PB, 978-1-59473-082-5 **$16.99**

JUDAISM

The Divine Feminine in Biblical Wisdom Literature
Selections Annotated & Explained
Translation & Annotation by Rabbi Rami Shapiro; Foreword by Rev. Cynthia Bourgeault, PhD
Uses the Hebrew books of Psalms, Proverbs, Song of Songs, Ecclesiastes and Job,
Wisdom literature and the Wisdom of Solomon to clarify who Wisdom is.
5½ x 8½, 240 pp, Quality PB, 978-1-59473-109-9 **$16.99**

Ethics of the Sages: *Pirke Avot*—Annotated & Explained
Translation & Annotation by Rabbi Rami Shapiro Clarifies the ethical teachings of the
early Rabbis. 5½ x 8½, 192 pp, Quality PB, 978-1-59473-207-2 **$16.99**

Hasidic Tales: Annotated & Explained
Translation & Annotation by Rabbi Rami Shapiro
Introduces the legendary tales of the impassioned Hasidic rabbis, presenting them as
stories rather than as parables. 5½ x 8½, 240 pp, Quality PB, 978-1-893361-86-7 **$16.95**

The Hebrew Prophets: Selections Annotated & Explained
Translation & Annotation by Rabbi Rami Shapiro; Foreword by Zalman M. Schachter-Shalomi
Focuses on the central themes covered by all the Hebrew prophets.
5½ x 8½, 224 pp, Quality PB, 978-1-59473-037-5 **$16.99**

Zohar: Annotated & Explained *Translation & Annotation by Daniel C. Matt*
The best-selling author of *The Essential Kabbalah* brings together in one place the most
important teachings of the Zohar, the canonical text of Jewish mystical tradition.
5½ x 8½, 176 pp, Quality PB, 978-1-893361-51-5 **$15.99**

EASTERN RELIGIONS

Bhagavad Gita: Annotated & Explained *Translation by Shri Purohit Swami*
Annotation by Kendra Crossen Burroughs Explains references and philosophical terms,
shares the interpretations of famous spiritual leaders and scholars, and more.
5½ x 8½, 192 pp, Quality PB, 978-1-893361-28-7 **$16.95**

Dhammapada: Annotated & Explained *Translation by Max Müller and revised by*
Jack Maguire; Annotation by Jack Maguire Contains all of Buddhism's key teachings.
5½ x 8½, 160 pp, b/w photos, Quality PB, 978-1-893361-42-3 **$14.95**

Rumi and Islam: Selections from His Stories, Poems, and Discourses—
Annotated & Explained *Translation & Annotation by Ibrahim Gamard*
Focuses on Rumi's place within the Sufi tradition of Islam, providing insight into
the mystical side of the religion. 5½ x 8½, 240 pp, Quality PB, 978-1-59473-002-3 **$15.99**

Selections from the Gospel of Sri Ramakrishna: Annotated & Explained
Translation by Swami Nikhilananda; Annotation by Kendra Crossen Burroughs
Introduces the fascinating world of the Indian mystic and the universal appeal
of his message. 5½ x 8½, 240 pp, b/w photos, Quality PB, 978-1-893361-46-1 **$16.95**

Tao Te Ching: Annotated & Explained *Translation & Annotation by Derek Lin*
Foreword by Lama Surya Das Introduces an Eastern classic in an accessible, poetic
and completely original way. 5½ x 8½, 192 pp, Quality PB, 978-1-59473-204-1 **$16.99**

About SKYLIGHT PATHS Publishing

SkyLight Paths Publishing is creating a place where people of different spiritual traditions come together for challenge and inspiration, a place where we can help each other understand the mystery that lies at the heart of our existence.

Through spirituality, our religious beliefs are increasingly becoming a part of our lives—rather than *apart* from our lives. While many of us may be more interested than ever in spiritual growth, we may be less firmly planted in traditional religion. Yet, we do want to deepen our relationship to the sacred, to learn from our own as well as from other faith traditions, and to practice in new ways.

SkyLight Paths sees both believers and seekers as a community that increasingly transcends traditional boundaries of religion and denomination—people wanting to learn from each other, *walking together, finding the way.*

For your information and convenience, at the back of this book we have provided a list of other SkyLight Paths books you might find interesting and useful. They cover the following subjects:

Buddhism / Zen	Gnosticism	Mysticism
Catholicism	Hinduism /	Poetry
Children's Books	Vedanta	Prayer
Christianity	Inspiration	Religious Etiquette
Comparative	Islam / Sufism	Retirement
Religion	Judaism / Kabbalah /	Spiritual Biography
Current Events	Enneagram	Spiritual Direction
Earth-Based	Meditation	Spirituality
Spirituality	Midrash Fiction	Women's Interest
Global Spiritual	Monasticism	Worship
Perspectives		

Or phone, fax, mail or e-mail to: SKYLIGHT PATHS Publishing
Sunset Farm Offices, Route 4 • P.O. Box 237 • Woodstock, Vermont 05091
Tel: (802) 457-4000 • Fax: (802) 457-4004 • www.skylightpaths.com
Credit card orders: (800) 962-4544 (8:30AM–5:30PM ET Monday–Friday)
Generous discounts on quantity orders. SATISFACTION GUARANTEED. Prices subject to change.